Mike Leigh

ECSTASY

NICK HERN BOOKS
London

A Nick Hern Book

Ecstasy first published in 1989 as an original paperback
by Nick Hern Books. This edition first published in 1996
by Nick Hern Books, 14 Larden Road, London W3 7ST

Front cover illustration of Mike Leigh by Antony Sher,
'Another Session' crayons, 1980. Reproduced with permission

Typeset by Book Ens, Saffron Walden, Essex
Printed by Athenaeum Press Ltd, Gateshead, Tyne and Wear

ISBN 1 85459 321 8

A CIP catalogue record for this book is available from the
British Library

Characters

JEAN
ROY
DAWN
VAL
LEN
MICK

Jean and Dawn are natives of Birmingham. Mick is from County Cork, Len is from rural Lincolnshire and Roy and Val are from inner North London, where the play is set. The dialogue, language and usage in *Ecstasy* are extremely precise, and in the author's view the play should only be performed in the correct accents.

Time: 1979

Ecstasy was first performed at the Hampstead Theatre, London, on 19 September 1979 with the following cast:

JEAN	Sheila Kelley
ROY	Ron Cook
DAWN	Julie Walters
VAL	Rachel Davies
LEN	Jim Broadbent
MICK	Stephen Rea

Directed by Mike Leigh
Designed by Alison Chitty
Costumes by Lindy Hemming
Lighting by Alan O'Toole

ACT ONE

Scene One

JEAN's bedsitting room in Kilburn. Bleak. Cramped. Kitchen within the room, concealed behind crude wall-partition, in doorway of which is old, disused 'Marley' folding door. Main room entered through kitchen. Furniture all drab, second-hand. Single bed, wardrobe (kept closed), small armchair, table (more cluttered than used), two chairs (one by the table, one serving as a bed-side table), bed-side lamp, alarm-clock, one-bar electric fire, mirror, old television set (in little-used position), old record-player, old transistor radio, paperback books, newspapers, box of chocolates, empty bottles, candle in wine bottle, cigarette packets, matches, some dead flowers in a jug, odds and ends. In the kitchen, an old 'Baby Belling' electric cooker, small sink, 'Sadia' (or similar) electric water heater, electricity meter, electric kettle, pans, shelves, garbage-bin, tins of food, culinary odds and ends.

Night, winter.

Lights up.

JEAN and ROY, stark naked on the bed. JEAN is lying on her back. ROY is sitting sideways on the bed, with his back to her. Neither moves.

Pause.

ROY picks up a packet of cigarettes, and takes one out.

ROY. Wanna fag?

JEAN. Yeah.

> *ROY gives her a cigarette, then lights the cigarettes, his own first.*

ROY. Good that, wannit?

JEAN. Yeah.

> *ROY gets up, goes to the table, picks up an opened can of beer, and finishes it off in one. Then he puts on his underpants, takes a fresh can of beer out of a carrier-bag, and opens it.*

ROY. You want one of these?

JEAN. No.

> JEAN *gets dressed.* ROY *drinks.*
>
> ROY *belches.*
>
> JEAN *makes the bed. Then she picks up an almost-empty Martini bottle from the floor near the bed, pours the last drop into an empty glass, and puts the bottle back on the floor.*
>
> ROY *gets dressed.*
>
> JEAN *sits in the armchair.*

JEAN. I 'ate the winter.

ROY. Still cold, are you?

JEAN. Yeah – ain't you?

ROY. Me? No.

> JEAN *puts on a cardigan.*
>
> ROY *is finishing tying his shoelaces. He glances at his watch.*

JEAN. What's the time?

ROY. Ten past nine.

> JEAN *gets up and goes into the kitchen.*

JEAN. I'll put the kettle on.

> *She does so.*
>
> Do you want a cup o' tea?
>
> ROY *finishes the can of beer.*
>
> Eh?
>
> ROY *adjusts his crutch.*
>
> D'you want a cup?
>
> *Pause.*
>
> You going?

ROY. Yeah, I got to shoot off.

JEAN. Why?

ROY. 'Cos I 'ave.

JEAN. Oh, sorry.

Pause.

ROY. 'Ere, you can 'ave them.

JEAN. What?

ROY. Some bee's left.

JEAN. Thanks.

ROY. Tara. 'Ere – 's a good job your friend didn't turn up, eh?

JEAN. Well, it's still early yet, 'er still might come.

ROY. Yeah, well. See you.

> ROY *leaves.*

> JEAN *takes an unopened can of beer out of the carrier-bag, and puts several empty cans and the Martini bottle into the carrier-bag, which she puts by the garbage can in the kitchen. She unplugs the kettle. Then she goes to the wardrobe, opens it, gets out a new bottle of Martini, and puts that on the table. Then she closes the wardrobe, and tops up her drink from the new bottle, which she puts on the floor where the old one was. She sits on the bed, and puts her glass on the chair by the bed. She gets the can of beer from the table, and puts that on the chair by the bed. She puts her feet up on the bed, and has a swig of Martini.*

> *Pause.*

> *Blackout.*

End of Scene One

Scene Two

Early evening, winter.

Lights up – dim: the room unlit.

JEAN *heard opening the front door. Children's voices heard in the street.*

DAWN (*off*). Tracy! Mind that bleedin' lamp-post, will ya? And keep away from that kerb! Told ya.

JEAN (*entering the room*). Init dark?

> JEAN *turns on the light.*

DAWN (*entering*). Listen to a word you bleedin' say they don't, Jean. Jean –

JEAN. Mm?

DAWN. Can I leave this door open a bit?

JEAN. Yeah, alright.

DAWN. Bleedin' cloth ears, them two, talk yourself stupid, you would.

JEAN. Been waitin' out there long, 'ave yer?

DAWN. No, no. I've 'ad 'em up to 'ere today, Jean, up to 'ere.

JEAN. 'Ave yer?

DAWN. I 'ave. Drove me mad. Blimey, it's parky, init?

JEAN. I'm just plugging the fire in.

DAWN. Been up Oxford Street today.

JEAN. 'Ave yer?

DAWN. Yeah. They'm buggers, y'see, Jean. Buggers! Murder comin' up the Kilburn 'Igh Road with them!

JEAN is offering DAWN a cigarette.

No, come on, 'ave one o'mine.

JEAN. 'Ere no, 'ave one o' these.

DAWN. Don't be so daft – come on.

JEAN. Go on. I've got them out now.

DAWN. Oh, go on, then. Jesus, 'er's got a mouth on 'er, Tracy. No discipline you see, Jean. What it is, no bleedin' discipline. 'E ain't no 'elp, neither – all on my back, you know.

JEAN is putting on the kettle in the kitchen.

JEAN. Mm.

DAWN. Jean . . .

JEAN. Aye?

DAWN. Fancy goin' out tomorrow night?

Pause.

JEAN. Yeah.

DAWN. Do ya?

JEAN. Yeah.

DAWN. Go for a drink, eh? Me and you?

JEAN. Yeah.

DAWN. Yeah. Thought we'd go to the 'Bell'.

JEAN. Mm.

DAWN. Yeah. 'E'll be there, mind.

JEAN. Will 'e?

DAWN. Oh, don't matter, though, Jean, don't 'ave to drink with 'im.

JEAN *laughs.*

Children's voices in street.

DAWN. 'Er upstairs'll baby-sit.

JEAN. Will 'er?

DAWN. Oh, ah. Better go an' check 'em, Jean, see if they'm alright – I couldn't mek it last night, you know.

DAWN *is on the way out.*

JEAN. No.

DAWN. No – wouldn't stop in, would 'e?

JEAN *laughs.*

Pause.

DAWN *returns.*

DAWN. 'Er's soaked, Michelle, y'know, needs changing. Ooh, Jean, I've 'ad a week of it with them two and that push-chair.

JEAN. 'Ave yer?

DAWN. They both want to push the babby now – both on 'em, Simone an' all – fighting, they've bin, told 'er, 'Tracy pushes the push-chair, not Simone. Tracy knows.' Don't like it, though, y'know, Simone – don't like bein' told. 'E bought 'er a little doll's pram, see, for 'er birthday, that's what started it, Jean.

JEAN. Oh, ah.

DAWN. Told 'er, 'Michelle ain't no doll. Proper babby. No doll.'

JEAN. Got a present for 'er 'ere.

JEAN gets out a paper bag.

DAWN. Don't deserve no present, 'er, Jean.

JEAN. 'Ere y' are.

DAWN. You bought 'er?

JEAN. Paintin' book and some paints.

DAWN. 'Er ain't gettin' that tonight – you know what 'er's been doin', Jean?

JEAN. No.

DAWN. 'Er's only been goin' round at school tellin' everybody 'er Daddy's died. Daddy's died, Jean! Says, 'I'll give you died, Simone, give you died! – See if 'e's died when 'e comes in tonight!'

JEAN. 'E wouldn't like that, will 'e?

DAWN. 'E wouldn't like it, Jean! Thinks the sun shines out of 'er, 'e does. Favouritises 'er, see, t'ain't right. No, 'er was waitin' for me tonight, teacher at the school gates, when I went to pick 'em up – oh, ah: Miss Beaumont-Lewis. Said 'er was worried about Simone. I said, 'Oh, you're worried, am ya, worried?' I says, 'you wanna 'ave the three on 'em, then you'd be worried!' Said 'er was subvertive.

JEAN. Eh?

DAWN. Said Simone was subvertive.

JEAN. Perhaps somebody in the class, their Dad's died, 'er's just copying them.

DAWN. Must 'ave, Jean.

JEAN. Yeah, that'd be it.

DAWN. Must 'ave – they do that, see? 'M buggers. 'Ey – got yer a present.

JEAN. 'Ave yer?

DAWN. Yeah: top.

DAWN produces a brightly coloured 'top' – i.e. blouse etc.

JEAN. Ooh.

DAWN. Lovely, init?

JEAN. Yes, 't's nice.

DAWN. Thought of you when I seen that, Jean. Got me one, an' all.

JEAN. 'Ave yer?

DAWN (*producing an identical 'top'*). See?

JEAN. Oh, ah.

DAWN. Lovely, in't they?

JEAN. Yeah, nice colours, in't they?

DAWN. Eh? Ooh, ah! Seen this, Jean, I said, 'It's goin' on my back, that is.'

JEAN. Did you buy 'em?

DAWN. 'Course I did – did I fuck! Did I buy 'em? Yer'm jokin', in't ya?

JEAN. Yeah.

DAWN. Did I buy 'em! Got 'em up C & A. Don't buy nothin' in C & A, you go in, 'elp yourself. See, got me a skirt, an' all.

JEAN. Oh, ah.

DAWN. Lovely, enit?

JEAN. Yeah, it's nice.

DAWN. See – it's got a pleat.

JEAN. Oh, ah.

DAWN. See what I mean, you can wear 'em together.

JEAN. Yeah. Yeah, it'll suit you, that.

DAWN. Ooh, ah. I 'ope they'll fit me, though, Jean. Ent tried 'em on, you know. Tell ya – if these don't fit me, I'm takin' them back.

JEAN. Ooh, blimey.

Pause.

DAWN. Been to work, 'ave ya?

JEAN. Yeah.

Pause.

DAWN. Busy, was ya?

JEAN. Yeah.

Pause.

DAWN. Been doin' wi' yourself?

JEAN. Just goin' to work, and coming home, yer know . . .

DAWN. Ent yer been out nowhere?

JEAN. No.

DAWN. Ooh, Jean, that ent no good for ya.

JEAN. Oh well, suits me, that.

DAWN. You still ent got a bloke?

JEAN. No.

    JEAN *goes into the kitchen to make the tea.*

DAWN. Oh, Jean, you wanna get yourself a nice bloke, you do, get yourself took out.

JEAN. 'T's easier said than done, init?

DAWN. Oh, ar, I know. Never mind, Jean, go out tomorrow night, get yourself pissed.

    JEAN *laughs.*

    Did I tell yer Tracy got thrown out of Irish Dancing Class?

JEAN. No.

DAWN. Did, you know; last Sat'day.

JEAN. What for?

DAWN. Tell you what for, Jean – I'll tell you what 'er told me. 'Er was doin' the dancing, right?

JEAN. Mm.

DAWN. An' there was this little kid dancin' be'ind 'er, Mickey Lynch. Trod on 'er shoe, see? So, 'er come out o' the shoe, an' 'er couldn't do the dancin' proper, the teacher was goin' on at 'er. Jean: 'er only turned round an' punched 'im in the throat; called 'im an Irish cunt.

JEAN. Ooh dear.

DAWN. No, it's that Miss Beaumont-Lewis I can't stick, though, Jean. Can't stick 'er, I can't. Looks down on me – know what I mean?

JEAN. Yeah.

DAWN. Can tell. Thinks I don't know. Snob, 'er is. Wooden bleedin' earrings, Jean.

JEAN gives DAWN a cup of tea.

Ooh, lovely. Lovely, Jean. Ent you been out with nobody?

JEAN is smuggling ROY's can of beer into the kitchen.

JEAN. No, no. Old is 'er, that teacher?

DAWN. Eh? Oh, I don't know – 'er's older 'n' us. Int married, though, int got no babbies. Think they'm it, teachers.

JEAN sits at the table with her tea.

JEAN. Ooh, ah, they're all the same, int they?

DAWN. Ooh, ah.

JEAN. D'you remember Sister Boniface?

DAWN. Ooh, blimey, I do. I 'ated 'er, I did!

JEAN. And Mrs Malvern.

DAWN. Ooh, ar, 'er 'ated me.

JEAN. 'Er weren't too fond of me, either.

DAWN. 'Er worn't, was 'er? 'T's lovely, that top, though, init, Jean?

JEAN. Oh, yeah.

DAWN. You wanna wear that tomorrow night, you do.

JEAN. Yes.

DAWN. Do yourself up a bit.

JEAN. Oh, well, I'm alright, you know . . .

DAWN. No, you wanna enjoy yourself, you do, Jean.

JEAN. Yeah. Wanna fag?

DAWN. No, come on – 'ave one o' mine, 'ad one o' yourn.

JEAN. Is Mick workin'?

DAWN. Eh? Ooh, ah, 'e's workin' today, in 'e? Wunt workin' last Friday, though. Celebrating Simone's birthday, see, Thursday night.

JEAN. Ooh, ah.

DAWN. Gave 'er a bit of a party, I did. Got 'er a little cake, few candles for the top. Little Eamonn come down, from upstairs – Theresa bought 'er a bunny rabbit, Jean – bunny rabbit, an' 'er's six. Stupid – any road, Michelle went and dropped it down the toilet, 'ad to throw it out. Bumped 'er 'ead on that basin an' all again you know, Jean.

JEAN. Mm?

DAWN. 'S got bumps on 'er 'ead the size of eggs. You know that cupboard in our kitchen that don't shut?

JEAN. Yeah.

DAWN. Always goin' into it.

JEAN. Comes sharp that, an' all, dunnit?

DAWN. Ooh ah. Any road, as I say, 'e comes in, Jean, gives 'er 'er doll's pram, 'e goes out. Don't see 'im till three o'clock Friday morning. Wouldn't go to work then, see? Sat'day, twelve o'clock, Jimmy the Gimp comes round, they go out, don't see 'im till all hours Sunday morning; throwin' up everywhere 'e was, an' all. Said it was the curry! Y'know what I mean?

JEAN. Oh ah.

DAWN. Yeah – made me laugh, though, Jean. Couldn't get up the pub all day Sunday. Too poorly, see? Din't go in Monday, neither.

JEAN. Did yer get me card?

DAWN. Ooh ah. Got yer card, ah! 'Er were dead chuffed wi' that, Simone. Card? Auntie Jean? Ooh, ah. Should've come round over the weekend, Jean.

JEAN. Yeah. Yeah, well – I 'ad a lot to do, you know.

DAWN. Did yer? What was yer doin'?

JEAN. Well, I 'ad to clean the place up a bit. Give the 'all a bit of a scrub – Sunday's the only day you've got to do it, init?

DAWN. Ooh ah, I know, don't tell me. You doin' tonight?

JEAN. Well, probably watch the telly, 'ave a bath, give me 'air a bit of a wash, you know . . .

DAWN. Yeah. There's a funny smell in 'ere, you know, Jean.

JEAN. Of what?

DAWN. Dunno – 's a funny smell, though.

JEAN. It's probably the cigarettes.

DAWN. No – don't smell like cigarettes to me.

JEAN. Well, I can't smell anything.

DAWN. No, you live 'ere, don't ya?

JEAN. 'T's right.

DAWN. No – can't smell your own place, see? Should've got me some tights, an' all. 'T's alright that skirt, though, init, Jean?

JEAN. Yeah, 't's nice.

DAWN. They've got some gorgeous stuff in C & A, though.

JEAN. Yeah, good shop, C & A.

DAWN. Ooh, ah. Get you a skirt if you want, Jean.

JEAN. Well, I don't really need any skirts.

DAWN. Don't ya? Int yer been nowhere, Jean?

JEAN. No, no. Well, you can't go out on yer own, can yer?

DAWN. No, you can't, no. Think you'm on the make, don't they? Know what men'm like, Jean. Only after one bleedin' thing. Eh?

JEAN. Mm.

DAWN. Better be goin', any road.

JEAN. Yeah, got to get their teas.

DAWN. Yeah, beefburgers I've got 'em – Jesus, 'er's got an appetite on 'er, Tracy – 'er eats more'n 'e does, 'er does, Jean – size on 'er, an' all.

JEAN. 'Er's only thin, in' er?

DAWN. 'Er is. Worries me, you know, that does. Think 'er's got a worm, I do. I mean, look at Simone: 'er's well-rounded, Simone, 'er don't eat 'alf as much as Tracy – 'alf a pound of bleedin' sugar 'er put on 'er Sugar Puffs this morning, Jean, three spoons o' sugar in 'er tea, I say to 'er, 'You'll be gettin' sugar diabetes next, you.' No, I'll get 'em to bed, though, Jean, tomorra. Mind you, 'er's a bugger, Tracy, you know, she still ain't sleepin' proper.

JEAN. Per'aps 'er just don't need a lot o' sleep.

DAWN. No, 'er ain't like you. Think it's nerves, I do. Little bags under 'er eyes, 'n' all, y'know, I says, 'You'll be moaning about them when you'm eighteen – come to me wi' bags under your eyes an' no teeth!' Not 'avin' that tomorrow night, though, Jean: get 'em to bed. Mind you, they'll go to bed, you know what I mean, they'll go. They'm'll say their prayers every night, you know, Tracy and Simone, ooh ah, kneel down, 'God Bless Mummy, God Bless Daddy, God Bless Tracy, God Bless Simone, God Bless Michelle, God Bless Mickey Mouse, God Bless Auntie Jean,' you'm 'alf-way out o' the bleedin' door, Jean, and they'm up. Cunts. You fancy a night out, though, do ya?

JEAN. Oh, yeah. Yeah.

DAWN. You ain't been out wi' nobody?

JEAN. No. No – I ain't met anybody I've liked.

DAWN. Oh; ain't there no blokes down that garage, Jean?

JEAN. Well, only them I work with.

DAWN. Oh ah, they'm Pakis, ent they?

JEAN. Yeah.

DAWN. You don't want to be goin' out wi' them, Jean.

JEAN. Don't I?

DAWN (*going out*). You wanna get this door shut, Jean, get the flat warmed up a bit.

JEAN. Ar, I will.

JEAN *sees* DAWN *to the hall*

DAWN (*off*). Yeah. Pick you up tomorrow, Jean, eight-thirty: alright?

JEAN (*off*). Alright.

DAWN (*off*). Yeah. See where buggers've got to now.

JEAN (*off*). Tara a bit.

JEAN *comes back into the room.*

DAWN (*off*). Tara, Jean. Tracy! Come on, we'm going! Simone.

Children's voices. DAWN *closes the front door.*

JEAN *takes the evening newspaper and a fresh packet of cigarettes out of her shopping-bag, and puts the bag in the kitchen. Then she goes to the wardrobe, gets out a bottle of gin, and puts it on the table. She hangs the new 'top' on a clothes-hanger in the wardrobe. She closes the wardrobe. She puts the dirty tea-cups in the kitchen sink, out of which she takes a dirty glass. She washes this, comes back into the room, sits at the table, and pours herself a gin.*

She doesn't drink it. She doesn't do anything.

Pause.

Blackout.

End of Scene Two

Scene Three

Evening.

Lights up.

JEAN *is sitting on the bed, reading a newspaper. The bed-side lamp is on. She is wearing a different-coloured cardigan. Her feet are on the floor.*

She puts down the newspaper, and sits back on the bed, with her feet up. She picks up the clock, looks at it, and puts it back. (It's well after 9 o'clock.)

She gets up, goes into the kitchen, takes a dirty glass from the sink, washes and dries it, comes back into the room, gets a bottle of tonic water from the wardrobe, and pours herself a gin-and-tonic.

She stands sipping her drink. Then she lights the candle. Then she gets out a cigarette, and lights it from the candle.

Pause: she stands, looking at the candle.

Then she puts the cigarettes, the matches, and an ashtray by the armchair, gets her drink, sits down, and starts reading a paperback book. Then she kicks off her shoes.

The door-bell rings.

Pause.

JEAN *gets up and goes to the front door.*

ROY (*off*). Hullo, Jean. Thought I'd come round and see 'ow you was, you know?

JEAN (*off*). Yeah.

> *They come into the room.*

> Come in.

ROY. 'Ow are you, are you alright?

JEAN. Yeah, yeah, I'm alright, are you?

ROY. Want a fag?

JEAN. No, I've got one on, ta.

ROY. What's that you're drinking?

JEAN. Gin-and-tonic: d'you want one?

ROY. No thanks. Ain't there none of my beer left?

JEAN. Yeah.

> JEAN *gets* ROY's *can of beer from the kitchen.*

ROY. Ta.

> ROY *opens the beer.*

> 'Ow are you, are you alright?

> JEAN *is back in the kitchen, cleaning another glass.*

JEAN. Yeah, yeah. Glass 'ere.

ROY. Bit of a change, init, gin-and-tonic?

JEAN. Yeah – yeah, well, I like a change, sometimes.

> JEAN *sits back in the armchair.* ROY *sits on the bed.*

> *Pause.*

ROY. 'Ow yer been, alright?

JEAN. Yeah. You been up the pub?

ROY. Yeah, popped in for a couple, you know . . .

> *Pause.*

> You go out last night?

JEAN. No.

ROY. Oh, I should've come round. What you been doin', then?

JEAN. Just workin'. You still doin' that Indian Restaurant?

ROY. No, got shot of that.

JEAN. What you doin' now, then?

ROY. 'Ouse.

JEAN. Where?

ROY. Up in 'Ampstead. Big fuckin' palace of a place.

JEAN. Bet that's cold, init?

ROY. What?

JEAN. Paintin'.

ROY. No, we're doin' the insides. Do exteriors when they get
    back.

JEAN. Where they gone?

ROY. South Africa.

JEAN. Well, they must trust you, then, if they've left you there on
    your own.

ROY. Do they fuck. They'll 'ave someone round to keep an eye
    on us, relation or something.

> *Pause.*

> Wondered if you'd be in. You know . . .

JEAN. Yeah. Yeah – well I am.

ROY. Warm enough over there for you?

JEAN. Yeah. Yeah.

ROY. Still got the old candle on, then?

JEAN. Yeah. Saves the matches.

ROY. Burn the fuckin' place down, you will.

Pause. Then ROY *gets up, and takes a swig of beer.*

ROY. Thought I'd come round 'n' see 'ow you was, you know.

JEAN. Yeah – well, I'm alright.

ROY *picks up a book.*

ROY. Still readin' then?

JEAN. Yeah.

ROY. Fuckin' waste of time.

He throws the books on the bed. Then he sits on the corner of the bed, nearer to JEAN.

Pause.

JEAN (*getting up*). I think I'll get a top-up.

ROY. You seen your friend?

JEAN. Yeah.

ROY. What, she turn up?

JEAN. No, 'er come yesterday. Why?

ROY. Oh, I wondered why she didn't come.

JEAN. Couldn't.

ROY. Why's that?

JEAN. Couldn't get a babysitter.

ROY. Oh, yeah: fuckin' kids.

JEAN (*sitting in the armchair*). Don't seem to keep you in.

ROY. Eh? 'T's not my problem, is it?

JEAN. They're your kids.

ROY. I didn't fuckin' ask for them. What're them, then?

JEAN. Pistachio nuts – d'you want one?

ROY. No, thanks.

JEAN. Don't you like 'em?

ROY. No. What, are they sweet, are they?

JEAN. They're lovely – 'ave one.

ROY. No, they don't taste of nothing.

JEAN. 'Course they do.

ROY. Where d'you get 'em, then?

JEAN. Shop.

ROY (*rubbing* JEAN'*s leg*). Alright, are you?

JEAN. Yeah.

ROY. Get your legs burnt off, sittin' there.

JEAN. Oh, I don't care.

ROY. Goin' out the weekend?

JEAN. No. Are you?

ROY. Dunno yet. Might go up the Dogs. (*He takes the bag of pistachio nuts from* JEAN'*s lap*.) 'Ow much you pay for these, then?

JEAN. 75 pence.

ROY. Oh. Yeah. That's a lot, init, for peanuts?

JEAN. Well, they are expensive.

ROY (*tossing them back into her lap*). You've been done.

Pause.

You alright over there?

JEAN. Yeah – don't I look alright?

ROY. Come and sit over 'ere.

JEAN. No, I'm alright 'ere, I like it 'ere.

Pause. Then ROY *gets up, goes over to the empty bottles, and checks through them.*

ROY. Got any more beer left?

JEAN. No.

ROY. What, no Guinness?

JEAN. No.

He picks up the new Martini bottle.

ROY. Is this the same bottle?

JEAN. Yeah.

ROY. Cor, I 'ate gin. (*Pouring himself a gin.*) Want another one?

JEAN. No. I've just 'ad one. But you 'ave one.

ROY. Ta. Cheers.

ROY *lights a cigarette. He swigs his gin. He sits on the bed.*

ROY. 'Ere y'are, come on.

JEAN. No, I'm alright 'ere.

ROY *clears a newspaper off the bed.*

ROY. Still cold, are yer?

JEAN. Well, 't ain't warm, is it?

ROY *clears the book off the bed.*

ROY. 'Ere y'are: come and sit over 'ere.

JEAN. No.

ROY *gets up. He moves over to* JEAN, *and leans over her.*

ROY. Alright, are you?

JEAN. Yeah. Yeah.

ROY. You sure?

JEAN. Yeah. Mm.

ROY. 'Ere y'are, come and sit over 'ere.

He moves her across to the bed. They sit on the bed, side by side.

ROY. That's better, init?

JEAN. Yeah.

He kisses her, briefly. Then he caresses her hair, slightly brutally. She takes a sip of her drink. He takes her glass from her, and puts it on the table.

He rubs her back.

ROY. Alright, are you?

JEAN. Yeah.

He kisses her again, and they lie down together, whilst continuing to kiss. Then JEAN *sits up abruptly.*

JEAN. Look, um, I don't really feel like it.

ROY. What's the matter?

JEAN. Well, I just don't feel like it.

ROY. Why?

JEAN. 'Cos I don't.

ROY. 'Course you do.

He forces her down again. He kisses her. He fondles her breasts. She turns her head away from him.

JEAN. No!!

ROY (*persisting*). What's the matter with you?

He sits up.

Bit of a change of tune, init?

Pause.

'S alright the other nights, wonnit? Eh?

JEAN. Yeah. Yeah.

Pause.

ROY. You wanna drink?

JEAN. Yeah.

He goes to the table, and pours some drinks. She sits up. He gives her a drink.

JEAN. Ta.

ROY. I was goin' to bring some beers.

Long pause.

'Ere y'are, come on: get it down yer. (*He tries to take her glass from her, but she holds on to it.*)

JEAN. 'Aven't finished it yet.

ROY *lights a cigarette.*

JEAN *gets up suddenly, puts down her drink, and quickly takes off her cardigan.*

JEAN. Come on, then.

> JEAN *lies on the bed on her back.* ROY *takes off his shirt, puts out his cigarette, and sits on the bed.*

JEAN *(as he sits)*. Let's get it over with.

ROY. What's your fuckin' game, eh?

JEAN. Gerroff me!

ROY. Eh? What're you playin' at?

JEAN. Gerroff.

> *They struggle for some time, with increasing violence.*
>
> *Eventually* ROY *jumps up.*

ROY. What the fuck's the matter with you?

> *Pause.*
>
> ROY *sits in the armchair.*

ROY. Fuckin' bitches, you're all the bleedin' same. You wannit, then you don't wannit.

> *He lights a fresh cigarette.*

Wanna fag?

> *Pause.*

JEAN. No.

> *Pause.*
>
> ROY *throws* JEAN *a cigarette.*
>
> *Pause.*
>
> *He gets up, goes over to the bed, and lights her cigarette.*
>
> *He hovers about.*
>
> *The doorbell rings.*
>
> *Pause.*
>
> JEAN *gets up quickly, and goes out to answer the door.*
>
> ROY *sits in the armchair.*

DAWN *(off)*. Ooh, blimey, Jean, never thought I'd bleedin' get 'ere. Bet you thought I worn't comin', dint ya?

JEAN (*off*). Yeah.

DAWN (*off*). . . . eh?

JEAN (*off*). Yeah.

DAWN (*off*). 'E ent been 'ome, 'as 'e?

JEAN (*off*). Ant 'e?

> *By now,* DAWN *is preceding* JEAN *into the kitchen.*

DAWN. 'E ent been 'ome, I'll bleedin' murder 'im when I get 'old of 'im, Jean.

> *She sees* ROY.

> Ooh, fuck! (*Quietly.*) 'Oo's 'im?

JEAN (*quietly*). Go on.

DAWN (*quietly*). Eh?

JEAN (*quietly*). Go on in.

> DAWN *comes into the room proper, followed by* JEAN.

DAWN. 'Iya.

ROY. 'Ow d'yer do.

JEAN. This is Roy. This is Dawn. So, 'e 'ant been 'ome then?

> DAWN *gets out a cigarette.*

DAWN. 'As 'e fuck been 'ome, Jean, 'e ent. Went out dinner-time today, ent seen 'im since. Dint go to work, see? Couldn't get up – drinkin' till two a.m.

> ROY *lights* DAWN's *cigarette.*

DAWN. Oh, ta.

ROY. This your friend, then?

JEAN. Yeah.

DAWN. Gorreny money, Jean?

JEAN. Yeah.

DAWN. I'm short now, see? Twenty quid 'e give me, Jean, twenty quid to last me the week. Then 'e borrows 'alf on it back. Michelle ate a five-pound note.

JEAN. 'Er ate it?

DAWN. Well, I mean 'er dain't eat it, but 'er chewed it up into little bits. Could've shoved me bleedin' purse down 'er throat, I tell ya.

ROY. You got a babysitter, then?

DAWN. Eh?

ROY. You got a babysitter?

DAWN. Ooh, yes, thank you.

>*Pause.*

> Live upstairs, do ya?

ROY. No.

DAWN. Oh. Thought you might've done.

ROY. Well I don't.

DAWN. Oh.

>*Pause.*

> Where d'you live then?

ROY. Why?

DAWN. Eh?

ROY. Why?

DAWN. I'm asking, in' I?

ROY. Round the corner.

DAWN. Oh. Not far then.

ROY. No.

>*Pause.*

JEAN. Think I'll put me shoes on.

>*She does so.*

DAWN. Jesus, are you 'ot or summat?

JEAN. Eh?

DAWN. State of 'im, Jean.

JEAN. Oh.

DAWN. Froze, I am.

JEAN. 'Tis cold, init?

DAWN. 'Tis, init?

ROY. Come over by the fire, then.

DAWN. D'you mean?

ROY. 'T's warmer over 'ere.

DAWN. Ooh I'm alright 'ere, thank you.

ROY. Come on.

DAWN (*going*). Eh? (*As she passes in front of* ROY.) 'Scuse me.

JEAN. Why don't you sit 'ere, Dawn?

DAWN. Ooh, no, don't be so daft, Jean. I'm alright 'ere.

JEAN. Let Dawn sit there.

    Pause.

ROY (*getting up*). 'Ere y'are, come and sit 'ere.

DAWN. Oh. Thank you.

ROY. Want a drink, Dawn?

DAWN. Eh?

ROY. Wanna drink?

DAWN. Ooh ah, go on, I'll 'ave a little 'un – I don't want no gin, though; can't abide it.

ROY. What about Martini?

DAWN. Oh ah, go on, I'll 'ave that.

    ROY *pours* DAWN's *drink.*

ROY. 'Ere y'are.

DAWN. Ta.

JEAN. I thought we were goin' out.

DAWN. We am – I'm ready when you am, I am, Jean.

JEAN. Oh, only I'm ready now, see.

DAWN. Yeah, right.

    JEAN *and* DAWN *start to get ready.*

ROY. You never said you was goin' out.

JEAN. Oh, well you never asked me.

The doorbell rings.

DAWN. Oo's that?

JEAN. I dunno. 'T'ain't for me, I know that.

JEAN *goes out.*

DAWN (*picking up* ROY's *shirt from the floor*). Yours, init?

VAL (*off*). Where is 'e? Eh?

Another door in the hall being rattled.

Eh?

VAL *appears in the kitchen doorway.*

ROY. What the fuck are you doin' 'ere?

VAL *rushes at* ROY, *pushing* DAWN *out of her way.*

VAL. You fuckin' bastard!

DAWN. Oh my God, what's goin' on?

VAL *grabs* ROY, *and they start struggling. Then they fall on the bed, and have a violent fight for some time. During this, probably before they actually fall on the bed,* VAL *drops her purse, unconsciously and not obviously.*

The following should be taken as an approximation of VAL's *utterances during the fight.*

VAL (*approximately*). You bastard. Fuckin' comin' round 'ere, I fuckin' knew it, all the time I'm stuck round there with them, you cunt, night after fuckin' night, 'ow long you think I – shit, you, I'll . . . you think you, think you can get away with it, do you? Think you can just, eh? Eh? Don't you? Eh? You cunt, you fuckin' shit cunt.

ROY. For fuck's sake!

The fight has continued, and at some point one end of the bed has collapsed. Finally, ROY *has pinned* VAL *down, and is gripping her throat.*

VAL. Geroff me, gerroff – bastard!

DAWN. 'Ey. 'Ey, 'ey, 'ey, come on, come on, gerroff! Geroff!

ROY (*to* DAWN). Fuck off!

VAL *is now on the floor, coughing.* ROY *gets to his feet.*

DAWN. All right. Leave 'er alone!

ROY *picks up the Martini bottle, and wields it weapon-like.*

DAWN. Don't be so fuckin' stupid – put that down!

ROY. You mind your own fuckin' business!

DAWN. Mind your bleedin' mouth!

ROY. D'you want one?

DAWN. Oh, ah? You and 'oo? You want to fight, go in the fuckin' street.

ROY. Bollocks!

VAL. Go on, then, use it! Go on, what're you waitin' for, eh?

VAL *gets up, and starts towards* ROY.

You spineless little wanker!

DAWN. Now, now, don't be silly!

VAL. Keep your nose out of this, you!

VAL *pushes* DAWN *against the partition.*

DAWN. Fuckin' ell!

VAL (*to* ROY). I'll 'ave you!

ROY. Oh, yeah?

VAL. I'll fuckin' 'ave you where it 'urts.

ROY. You what?

VAL. In your pocket. And don't you fuckin' dare come 'ome, neither, 'cos you're never going to see them kids as long as you live!

VAL *rushes out through the kitchen.*

ROY. Where the fuck are they?

VAL *rushes back, dislodging the 'Marley' door, which crashes to the floor.*

VAL. 'Where are they?' Where are they! What the fuck do you care where they are, eh?

ROY. Well, I didn't want 'em!

VAL. No, nor did I!

ROY. You fuckin' 'ad 'em, though, dint you?

VAL. Yeah, and you're goin' to fuckin' pay for them, Goldenballs!

She rushes out.

ROY. PISS OFF!

VAL (*off*). UP YOURS! CUNT!

The front door slams.

Pause.

DAWN. Satisfied, am yer? You wanna watch where you'm bleedin' puttin' it, you do!

She goes out into the hall.

(*off.*) Jean! Jean . . .

ROY *puts down the bottle. Then he puts on his shirt, and does up the buttons. Then he takes a chocolate, throws the chocolate-box on the bed, grabs his cardigan, and walks out.*

The front door closes.

Pause.

DAWN (*off*). 'Old on. 'Old on. 'E's gone, Jean.

JEAN (*off*). Is it a mess in there?

DAWN (*off*). 'E's bust yer bed, Jean. Tell ya now. Bust yer bed. Don't matter, though, Jean.

DAWN *and* JEAN *come into the room,* DAWN *leading the way.* JEAN *is crying.*

DAWN. Stupid bugger. Coming round, smashing other people's places. Jesus, Jean. (*She surveys the scene.*) You can't sleep on that, Jean. Can't! You'll 'ave to come up ours. Mick'll mend that for ya. 'Tain't no bother. Get 'im round tonight, 'tain't no bother Jean. Oh, blimey, Jean, where do you find 'em? Eh? Crawl out the bleedin' woodwork, they do.

JEAN. I go lookin' for 'em specially, you know!

DAWN. I know you do, you got a bloody gift for it, you 'ave!

JEAN. Oh ah, they're all 'and-picked. It's the first thing I say to 'em, 'You goin' to come round and smash the place up?' – If they say yes, it's alright.

DAWN. Ooh, don't.

JEAN. Ooh, God – I thought the bloody lot'd 'a' gone, y'know –

DAWN. Could 'ave.

JEAN. – The telly, the record player and everything.

DAWN. I know, could 'ave – did you 'ear 'im?

JEAN. Yeah.

DAWN. Jesus, Jean, 'er come in 'ere like a madwoman! Thought 'er was goin' to kill 'im, I did. Went for 'er with a bottle, an' all, y'know.

JEAN. Did 'e?

DAWN. Did! (*She indicates the floor.*) You'd 'ave 'ad a murder on your 'ands then, see?

JEAN. 'Ey: I bet 'er thought you was me, eh?

DAWN. Ooh, blimey, 'er scared me, Jean. Sent me flyin' a couple of times, you know. 'Er was waitin' outside, 'er was, when I come in.

JEAN. Was 'er?

DAWN. 'Er must've knowed 'e was 'ere.

JEAN. Mm.

DAWN. Must've knowed it, see?

JEAN. I'll tell you summat, I'm bloody glad you're 'ere.

DAWN. Ooh, ah.

JEAN. Look at this door out 'ere.

DAWN. Ooh ah, 'er's bust yer curtain.

JEAN. Let's stick it in the 'all, eh, prop it up in the 'all?

DAWN. Aye.

JEAN. 'Cos I've never used the thing, anyway.

DAWN. No.

The following whilst they carry the 'Marley' door out into the hall.

DAWN. Tell you one thing, Jean.

JEAN. What?

DAWN. There'll be no tea for 'im when 'e gets in tonight.

JEAN. Ho, no.

DAWN. Eh? Smacked botty, straight to bed.

They come back into the room.

JEAN. Huh . . . it ain't too bad, really, is it?

DAWN. Could've been worse, Jean.

JEAN. Ooh, ah.

DAWN. Could 'ave.

They look round the room. The following two lines of dialogue may be initiated by DAWN *or* JEAN, *depending on who in performance finds the purse first – which may vary from performance to performance, owing to the necessarily erratic nature of the moment when* VAL *drops the purse. However,* JEAN *is preferable.*

JEAN/DAWN. 'Ey, 'ere's your purse 'ere.

DAWN/JEAN. That ain't my purse.

Pause.

JEAN. Ooh blimey . . .

DAWN. Oh Jesus, it's 'ers!

JEAN (*taking out coins*). 'Ere – stick this in yer pocket, we'll 'ave a bloody drink out of it.

DAWN. Oh, Jean . . .

JEAN. 'Ere, there's a note 'ere, 'n' all. (*A pound note.*)

DAWN. Cor blimey, 't's 'er 'ousekeepin'!

JEAN. 'Ere, I'll chuck this up the 'all.

DAWN. No – don't put it up the 'all, put it on the step, they'll be on the bleedin' bell again, Jean.

JEAN. Ooh ah.

DAWN. Ah, you don't want that.

JEAN. Ooh, come on, let's get up that pub – I'm goin' to 'ave a bleedin' double when I get up there.

DAWN. Ooh ah. Knew 'e was a cunt, Jean. Knew it, soon as I caught 'is eyes, that's 'ow you see, you see. Can't blame 'er, Jean, can't. Married man, see? 'Tain't right. 'Tain't!

JEAN. Ey: d'you think they'll still be out there when we go out?

DAWN. Don't matter, Jean! 'Tain't your bother.

JEAN. Ooh, it ain't 'alf!

DAWN. Course it ain't.

JEAN. I'll 'ave to put me dark glasses on, I should.

DAWN. Blimey!

JEAN. 'Ey, Dawn . . .

DAWN. Yeah?

JEAN. Listen: if Mick's in the pub . . .

DAWN. Yeah?

JEAN. Don't tell 'im what 'appened, will yer?

DAWN. Course I wun't!

JEAN. I mean, not while I'm there – you can tell 'im tomorrow if you want, I just don't want to talk about it tonight, I don't want to mention it.

DAWN. Course I wun't! Won't tell 'im at all if you don't want me to, Jean, don't be so daft!

JEAN. Oh well, 't's up to you. I'll put the fire out. (*She does so.*)

DAWN (*going out*). You got everything, Jean?

JEAN. Yeah.

DAWN. Keys? Fags?

JEAN. Keys. Fags. Right.

DAWN. Don't forget that kitchen light, Jean.

JEAN. Right.

She puts out the lights, and they go out to the street . . .

DAWN (*off*). Ooh blimey, 't's nippy.

JEAN (*off*). Go and 'ave a look-round, see if it's all clear.

DAWN (*further away*). Don't be daft. There'll be nobody there.

JEAN (*in the distance*). Let's make a quick dash for it.

> *Silence.*

> *Fade to blackout.*

> **End of Act One**

ACT TWO

Night.

Lights up – darkness.

Then, from the street, and hardly audible –

JEAN. 'Ere it is.

LEN. Oh, aye.

> *The front door is heard opening. Then –*

LEN. Shall I leave this door, Jean?

JEAN. Yeah, you can leave that for 'em, Len – they know where I am.

> JEAN *unlocks the door to her room.*

JEAN. Just put this on the catch. Come on in then, Len.

LEN (*coming in*). Thank you. Nice little kitchen.

JEAN. Yeah.

LEN. Oh – it's a nice room, Jean.

JEAN. Oh, well it's alright, you know . . .

LEN. It's smashing.

JEAN. Well, it's big enough for me, any road.

LEN. See you got yourself a telly.

JEAN. Yeah.

LEN. Oh, I see – they've partitioned it off.

JEAN. Oh, ah, they just slung that in.

LEN. Well that's 'andy, in't it? (*Laughing*.) I see! You'd 'ave a job sleeping in that, wouldn't you?

JEAN. Yeah – I'd 'ave all the blood rush to me 'ead, wouldn't I?

LEN. Aye, you would, wouldn't you, aye?

JEAN. I think what must've 'appened, Len, is the threads've gone on them legs up there –

LEN. Oh ah.

JEAN. – 'Cos it's been wobbling about all over the place for ages, and it just went bump tonight.

LEN. Oh.

JEAN. Right. Well, I'll put you a record on.

LEN. Aye, that'd be nice.

DAWN (*in the street*). Don't ring the bell, Mick.

The bell rings.

LEN. 'Ere they are.

MICK (*in hall*). 'Ullo, 'ullo!

DAWN (*in hall*). Wake the bleedin' 'ouse up!

MICK (*banging the partition*). Anyone at home, like?

LEN. 'Ey-up, Mick!

MICK. Here you are – got the ole carry-out.

LEN. Aye. Aye.

MICK. Hope there's enough, like.

LEN. Aye!

MICK *and* LEN *indulge in a brief bout of playful mock-boxing.*

MICK. You big bollocks!

LEN. 'Ey-up! 'Ey! 'Ey!

DAWN. Wake the bleedin' dead, wouldn't 'e, Jean?

MICK. Right, Jean: couple o' glasses and we're away.

JEAN. Right.

DAWN. Eh? No, no, no, no, come on: before you start, get this bed mended first.

MICK. Oh, for Jesus' sake!

DAWN. Don't start, Mick: you said you'd do it!

MICK. Can we have a drink first, like?

DAWN. You 'ave any more to drink you won't be in no state to mend nothing!

MICK. Eh, anything for a quiet life.

(The following dialogue runs simultaneously with some of the preceding, and begins as MICK *is saying: 'Oh, for Jesus' sake'.)*

LEN. I'll be alright out the can, Jean, don't worry about me.

JEAN. I'll just give 'em a swill, Len.

LEN. Aye.

MICK. *(Eh, anything for a quiet life.)*
Let's have a look at the bed; Jean, what's the problems with the old bed?

DAWN. 'M legs'm bust, in't they, Jean?

JEAN. Yeah.

MICK. Sorry, Dawn, I beg your pardon, 'tis Jean I'm talking to, 'tis her who knows.

DAWN. I'm tellin' you, en' I?

MICK. 'Tis her bed, she knows the problems – Jean?

JEAN. Well, I think the threads've gone on them legs up there, see?

DAWN. That's right.

MICK. Threads have gone on the legs, Len.

LEN. Aye. Aye.

MICK. Okay, we'll have a look at that, no problem.

LEN. Right-o.

MICK *and* LEN *inspect the bed.*

MICK. Oh yeah, I see, yeah, yeah.

JEAN. Yes, best thing to do is to take these legs off 'ere, an' then we can 'ave it on the floor.

DAWN (*joining in with* JEAN). The floor, yeah, Mick, 'er wants these –

MICK. Ah, don't give me a pain in the ear.

DAWN. } I ent givin' you no pain in no ear.

MICK. } Grab the end of that there, Len.

LEN. Right-o, mate.

MICK. Throw it off here, like.

DAWN. Careful, careful!

MICK. Wait till I throw it – woa!

DAWN. Mind that fire!

MICK. Aw, for Jesus' sake, if you're not going to be any help, you can wait in the kitchen!

DAWN. Just tellin' you what 'er wants, 'en I?

MICK. Len – on its side, away from you.

LEN. Right-o mate: yonk it over!

They put the bed on its side; LEN *passes one of the bed-legs to* MICK.

LEN. 'Ere y'are, Mick.

MICK. Jesus, if you'd one like that, you could travel!

DAWN. 'Be rude!

LEN. No, this is completely split, you'll never get this leg in 'ere now, mate.

MICK. This hole here is bollocksed an' all, like.

DAWN. 'Course they am, 'er wants these'n's off, don't yer, Jean?

MICK. Ar, button it, will you?

DAWN. 'Tell me to button it!

MICK. Aye, there's been a weight on this bed.

DAWN (*quietly*). Shurrup, Mick, I've told you.

MICK. Kiss my arse.

DAWN. Oh ah.

(The following dialogue runs simultaneously with the preceding, and begins after: '. . . a weight on this bed.')

LEN. Is that what you want, then, Jean? Shall we whip these legs off?

JEAN. I think that'd be best, Len.

LEN. Right-o, then, whip these off.

MICK. Whip these buggers off.

They remove the remaining good legs. MICK *hands one to* DAWN.

MICK. Here: stick that in your mouth.

LEN. 'Ere y'are, Dawn, can you 'old these?

DAWN. Yeah.

MICK. And again. Right – let's get it back there, Len.

LEN. Alright, boy.

MICK. Woa!

JEAN. That lovely, thanks.

DAWN. 'T's alright, enit, Jean?

JEAN. Oh ah.

LEN. There. Let's have a drink.

JEAN. Thanks very much.

JEAN *and* DAWN *make the bed.*

JEAN. Don't worry about that, just cover it up.

DAWN. } No bother, Jean.
LEN. } What would you like, then, Jean?

JEAN. I'll have anything, Len.

MICK. Here, I have Jean's drink here. Jean: that's for you.

JEAN. Ooh, thanks very much.

MICK. Nice drop of Rin-Tin-Tin.

JEAN. Yeah.

LEN. Is that what you want, Jean?

JEAN. Ooh, I like a drop of gin, Len.

LEN. What would you like, Dawn?

DAWN. I'll 'ave a lager, please, Len.

LEN. Aye, right.

MICK. Here y'are, Missus, I have your drink here: that's for you.

DAWN. I don't want no vodka, Mick.

MICK. For fuck's sake, you've been drinking vodka all night.

DAWN. I know.

JEAN. We've got some tonic here, you know.

DAWN. Don't matter, Jean, don't want no vodka, thank you.

MICK. I bought that for you special, like.

DAWN. I told you not to, didn't I?

MICK. Ar, please yourself. Don't ask for it again – give her a lager, Len.

LEN. Is that what you want then, Dawn?

DAWN. Yes, please, Len – lovely.

LEN. 'Ere y'are, Dawn.

DAWN. Aw, lovely, 'kyou.

    JEAN *is in the kitchen.*

MICK. Don't suppose you've got an old rasher sandwich in there, Jean, eh?

JEAN. No, I int.

MICK. You haven't got a rasher?

JEAN. No.

MICK (*quietly to* DAWN). Fuck's sake, I thought you told me she'd have a rasher, like.

DAWN. Blimey, Mick, leave it alone, will ya?

JEAN. I got some bread, though.

MICK. Ah, no, you're okay, Jean, no. No problems – y'know.

DAWN. 'E's alright, Jean.

MICK (*quietly to* DAWN). I just thought there might be a fuckin' rasher in it.

DAWN (*quietly*). Aw, bleedin' stomach.

LEN. Nice place Jean's got 'ere, init?

DAWN. Too small for 'er, Len.

JEAN. It's alright, y'know.

LEN. Aye, it's small, but it's compact.

JEAN. Ah well, there ain't much to clean, that's what I like about it.

LEN. Aye, that's the main thing, intit?

DAWN. Tek me shoes off, Jean, 'scuse me.

LEN. Tek me jacket off, Dawn.

DAWN. Yeah – 'preciate the benefit, Len.

JEAN. Just stick that anywhere, Len.

LEN. Aye.

All four have now sat down.

LEN. Nice to see you all again, anyway.

JEAN. Yeah.

MICK. 'Tis fuckin' nice to see you an' all, boy.

LEN. Cheers, cheers!

DAWN. Lovely!

MICK. All the best!

LEN. Cheers, mate! Cheers, Jean!

JEAN. Cheers.

DAWN. Jean – bit of a shock for you, wor'n it, eh, Len?

LEN. It was a shock, it was a shock – that's why I didn't recognise you, Jean: I didn't expect to see you.

JEAN. No, I didn't expect to see you, either.

DAWN. 'Course yer didn't. Kept it secret, I did.

JEAN. Ah, you din' 'alf.

DAWN. I never said a word to 'er. Never said a word.

LEN. 'E never said a word to me.

MICK. No – there you are, you see, 'course, she would have it, Big-Mouth McSweeney would blow the whole bloody gaff, but – did I say a word to you, Len?

LEN. No, no – no – no – Dawn, Dawn –

DAWN. Yeah?

LEN. In all fairness to Mick, 'e dint say a word to me about it.

DAWN. Alright, alright, I believe you.

JEAN. 'Er never said nothing to me, either; 'er just said we'll go for a drink Friday night, so round 'er comes, up the pub we goes, and there you were. Weren' 'alf a shock!

LEN. Aye, a good'n, wo'n'tit?

DAWN. Jean, Jean: Tuesday night, 'e brings 'im 'ome; didn't know 'oo it was, Jean, did I? Didn't know 'oo it was.

MICK. No, I didn't know who it was, an' all on Tuesday night . . . I'm standing in the bar, taking my pint . . . (*He mimes a hand tapping on his shoulder*). 'Who the fuck is this?' like. Big smile all over his ugly old mug. 'I know that face. Fuckin' Hardwick!'

JEAN. You look ever so different, though, Len.

MICK. Ah, yeah, you've changed.

DAWN. No, 'e ain't changed!

LEN. Well, you get older, don't you?

DAWN. Only the glasses, Len.

MICK. We all get older, like.

LEN. Of course, you 'aven't seen me wi' glasses, 'ave you? – Well, that's the difference then, intit? Aye.

JEAN. Yeah.

DAWN. Been through it though, ent ya? Can tell, Len: see it in yer face.

LEN. Well, I've 'ad me ups and downs, but what with one thing and another, it evens itself out in the end, doesn't it?

JEAN. Yeah.

MICK. You're better off for it.

LEN. Yeah.

MICK. You're your own man – you can wake up in the morning, pack your bags, head off up the High Road, no bother on you.

LEN. Aye. Aye.

DAWN. Thanks very much, Mick: you know where the door is, don't you?

MICK. I wasn't fuckin' saying anything, like.

DAWN. You can see 'im bachelor gay, couldn't ya? Can't even boil an egg, you.

MICK. There's more to life than boiling eggs.

LEN. Now, now, Mick, I might be footloose and fancy free, but you're a lucky man, I'd give a lot to be in your shoes – you've got a nice flat, three lovely little girls – four lovely little girls with you, Dawn, if you don't mind me saying so.

DAWN. Ooh, blimey!

MICK. Aye, she's got a mouth on her you can hear at Marble Arch, like.

LEN. In some ways it's a surprise to see them two still together – d'you know what I mean, Jean?

JEAN. Ooh ah!

DAWN. Surprise to me, Len.

LEN. No, no, no, seriously, Dawn, we're 'avin' a joke now, but seriously, to see you two still together now, after all this time, so 'appy, and mekkin' something of your lives, well it warms my 'eart, and I just wanted to tell you that, anyway.

MICK (*getting up*). Put it there, Len baby – you're one of the best. Drink up, boy – go on.

JEAN. Yeah, let's 'ave a top-up.

DAWN. Ooh ah, Jean.

MICK. You were away a long while, but you weren't forgotten.

JEAN. 'Ere y'are.

DAWN. Ta, lovely, Jean.

LEN. I meant what I said, Mick, you know that, don't you?

MICK. I know that, Len-baby. From the heart. Aw Jesus, Jean, you've a snap here of the girls, eh?

LEN. Ooh, look, there they are, aye. Don't they look nice?

MICK. That's Tracy Dawn, like.

LEN. Oh, that's Tracy, is it?

MICK. Tracy.

DAWN. Tracy . . .

MICK. And that's Michelle, like.

LEN. Michelle – oh, doesn't she look lovely?

DAWN. Just about to start grizzling there, Len.

MICK. And that's my little favourite, Simone.

LEN. Simone, ah!

MICK. French name, like, you know . . .

MICK starts an asthma attack.

LEN. Aye. What's up, Mick? You alright?

JEAN. 'T's 'is asthma.

DAWN. Come 'ere to me.

LEN. Oh, 'e still gets 'is asthma, does 'e?

JEAN. Yes.

LEN. Oh dear.

DAWN. That's what 'e gets from drinking till two in the morning, Len.

LEN. Like a blockage, is it?

DAWN. No, it's alright, 'e's got 'is spray.

DAWN pounds MICK's back.

JEAN. They're nice kids, int they?

LEN. Aye, don't they look lovely?

JEAN. Mm . . . 'er's my favourite – Tracy.

LEN. Aye.

JEAN. 'Er's a character, 'er is.

LEN. Aye, got a cheeky little face, 'asn't she?

DAWN. Jean.

JEAN. Eh?

DAWN. Y'ain't got a packet o'soup, 'ave ya?

JEAN. Oh. I might 'ave.

DAWN. Eh? Only 't 'elps 'im, see, when 'e's like this.

MICK. 'Elps; you know . . .

JEAN (*suddenly remembering*). Ooh – I've got a tin of tomato soup.

DAWN. Lovely.

JEAN. D'you wannit now?

MICK. Jes', I wouldn't mind it now, Jean.

JEAN. Oh, alright.

DAWN. I'll mek it, Jean. I'll mek it.

JEAN. No, you sit yourself down.

DAWN. No bother.

JEAN. No, I'll just stick it on. Can I just come by 'ere, Len?

LEN. Sorry, Jean! Y'alright? There y'are.

JEAN. Oh, you didn't 'ave to move.

LEN. No, you're alright.

    Pause. JEAN *organises soup, saucepan, etc.*

LEN. You alright in there, Jean? D'you want a 'and, like?

JEAN. No, I'm alright, Len, thanks.

LEN. 'Ave your drink with yer, anyway. 'Ere y'are, 'ere's your drink.

JEAN. Thanks.

DAWN. Len.

LEN. Aye?

DAWN. D'you wanna fag?

LEN. Aye – don't mind if I do, Dawn, thank you.

DAWN. Jean.

JEAN. Eh?

DAWN. Wanna fag?

JEAN. Alright.

DAWN. Tek 'er a fag, Len.

LEN. I'll light it for 'er. I'll light it for you, Jean.

JEAN. Thanks, Len.

LEN. 'Ere y'are, Jean: lit it for you.

JEAN. Thanks Len.

LEN. Where's your toilet, Jean, if you don't mind me asking?

JEAN. Go out of 'ere, turn left, it's just the door on your right.

LEN (going). Right. Thank you.

JEAN. There's a light switch just in front of you there; just push it.

LEN (from hall). Oh, ah, aye. Thank you.

DAWN. Alright, am yer?

MICK. I'm alright.

DAWN. Should've got you tomato soup for your breakfast – might've got you to work.

MICK. Nobody eats tomato soup for their breakfast.

DAWN. Jean.

JEAN. Eh?

DAWN. Jean: it's a shame, intit? Shame, for Len.

JEAN. Oh; yeah.

DAWN. 'Is wife ran off an' left 'im, Jean.

JEAN. Yeah. 'E's been telling me.

DAWN. Told yer, yeah. Run off with a salesman. Been 'urt, 'e 'as.

JEAN. Yes, well anybody would be, wouldn't they?

DAWN. Ooh, ah. You couldn't do it to 'im, could yer, eh? Couldn't do it to 'im. 'E's that sort, though, see, Jean, gets 'urt easy.

MICK. Very soft-hearted.

DAWN. Ooh, ah, don't carry no airs.

MICK. No airs or graces.

DAWN. What's 'e say to you, Mick?

MICK. Eh?

DAWN. What's 'e say to you?

MICK. 'E didn't say fuck all to me.

DAWN. Ooh, blimey! You don't tell me nothing, you.

MICK. No, I don't poke my nose in there, Jean.

JEAN. No.

MICK. You know what I mean: what's passed is passed, that's his own affair, like.

JEAN. 'Tis. Yeah.

DAWN. No, but 'er must've been a flighty bit, though, Jean.

JEAN. Well, you don't know – you can't tell, can yer?

MICK. Don't suppose you got an old sausage to go along with the soup, Jean?

JEAN. No, I got nothing like that.

DAWN. Blimey, 't ain't no caffy, Mick. Ent done nothing but go on about 'is bleedin' stomach since 'e left that pub, Jean.

MICK. I was only asking. Am I out of order? Jean knows me.

DAWN. Ooh, ah, 'er knows you alright.

MICK. If I'm out of order, Jean'll tell me I'm out.

DAWN. 'Not sayin' you'm out of order.

MICK. Jean: am I out of order?

JEAN. No, no.

MICK. There you are, you see. Jean knows me. I didn't eat all day.

DAWN. Ooh, blimey, Mick, me 'eart bleeds for you – d'you 'ave enough to drink?

MICK. I'll have a rasher sandwich when I go home.

DAWN. You'll 'ave no rasher sandwich, you won't touch that bacon, you'll 'ave egg.

MICK. Didn't I have two egg sandwiches already today?

DAWN. That bacon's for breakfast.

LEN *returns*.

DAWN. Alright, am yer, Len?

LEN. Aye, ah: better out than in.

JEAN. 'T's a weight off your mind, init?

LEN. Aye.

DAWN. Enjoyed yourself tonight, ant yer?

LEN. Aye.

DAWN. Ey? – enjoyed yourself.

LEN. It's been a grand night.

MICK. It's been a great night.

JEAN. Yeah, it's been a good night.

LEN. Aye . . . Cheers, anyway.

JEAN. } Cheers!

DAWN. } Cheers!

MICK. All the very best.

LEN. You know, come back to London, it's a big old place, and after all this time, meeting up with you again, well, it's a bit unexpected really, intit? But you know, although there are so many people in London – well, there are thousands of 'em – millions, really, aren't there? – although there are so many, if you don't know anyone, it can be a bit lonely, to be quite frank with you.

DAWN. Oh, it can be very lonely, Len.

LEN. Aye. So, bumpin' into you again, and 'avin' a drink and a laugh, well it makes a big difference, and I do appreciate it, and I just wanted to tell you that, anyway.

MICK (*getting up*). Put it there, Len-baby.

LEN. Uh, Mick!

MICK. There you are, you see: this man's from Corby, and I'm from Cork, but we don't give a fuck. That was always our motto: Have A Drink, And Don't Give A Fuck!

DAWN. 'E ain't from Corby, Mick.

LEN. It dunt matter, Dawn.

MICK. What're you talking about?

DAWN. I'm talking about Len: 'e ain't from Corby.

MICK. Where's he from, then? I know this fuckin' man for years, and I'm telling you he's from Corby. 'Len From Corby.'

DAWN. 'Be stupid.

MICK. Len, you're a Corby man, aren't you – Jesus, I'll give you a pound note on it. There y'are! Len: where are you from?

LEN. You just lost yourself a quid, Mick: I'm not from Corby.

DAWN. Told ya.

JEAN. From Lincolnshire.

MICK. Ar, for Jesus' sake, you always told me you were from Corby.

LEN. No; no, what it was, Mick, before I came to London the first time, I worked in Corby.

MICK (*pocketing the pound*). There you are, you see – he worked in Corby, what am I telling you?

DAWN. Nothing to do with it!

MICK. 'Have A Drink, And Don't Give A Fuck', mm? Ah, that was always the way with us, yourself and meself, into every pub on the Kilburn High Road. (*Continues whispering into* LEN's *ear*.)

LEN (*laughing*). Aye!

MICK. Wild fuckin' men! They'd see us comin' a mile away. More money than sense.

LEN. Were younger, then, of course, weren't we?

MICK. We were younger then, of course, you see? I've seen the time I could sit down to eighteen or twenty pints, no bother on me. That was the way with us: money on the counter, get the pints down you, and hump the fuckin' begrudgers!!

DAWN. Jean, d'you wanna fag?

JEAN. Mm.

DAWN. Do ya? Alright, am ya?

JEAN. Yeah. Yeah.

DAWN. I'm froze, y'know.

JEAN. D'you wanna sit 'ere?

DAWN. No, pass us me coat.

JEAN. 'Ere y'are.

DAWN. Lovely, ta.

(*The following dialogue runs simultaneously with the preceding and carries on directly from: '. . . and hump the fuckin' begrudgers!!'*)

LEN. Then we'd go down the West End, occasionally, wouldn't we? Soho, down there.

MICK. Soho. Great place, the West End.

LEN. Aye.

MICK. I haven't been down there this years.

LEN. 'Aven't yer?

MICK. And then we'd roll home all hours of the fuckin' morning, like, back to the digs. Jean, we had this old digs up the road there, Mrs Clancy's –

JEAN. Yeah.

MICK. – We'd fall in the door four o'clock in the morning, pockets full of beer, 'Ssh-ssh!!' (*He bangs on the floor with his foot.*) 'If you boys don't keep quiet, you'll get no breakfast in the morning!'

LEN. Aye. Wonder what 'appened to 'er.

MICK. She's still up there.

LEN. Is she?

DAWN. Ooh, ah. 'E stayed with 'er, didn't you?

MICK. Oh, yeah: I stayed with her.

LEN. Did you?

MICK. Time Dawn's mother came down from Birmingham; time Michelle was born.

DAWN. Simone.

MICK. Was it Simone?

DAWN. 'Course it was Simone – Tennyson Road.

MICK. Oh, well. I stayed there for a couple of weeks, like. Very nice.

LEN. Mm.

MICK. Religious maniac.

LEN. Aye.

MICK. Off to Lourdes every five minutes, but very nice breakfast.

LEN. Aye, 't's a good a breakfast, I'll say that for 'er, did a good breakfast, aye.

Pause.

Wasn't she at your wedding?

MICK. Oh yeah. She was there.

LEN. Thought so.

MICK. Oh, Lord Jesus Christ, d'you remember the morning I got married?

DAWN. Ooh, blimey – don't!

MICK. Only for you giving me the big bumper of brandy to straighten meself out, I'd've never got anywhere near the church.

LEN. Aye, you were in a terrible state, Mick – you both were, you were an' all, Dawn. Jean, Jean, I'm surprised either of them can remember anything about that wedding-day, aren't you?

JEAN. Mm, yeah.

DAWN. Don't. Don't, Len – I don't remember me own wedding-day.

MICK. Jesus' sake, you must remember your wedding-day.

DAWN. No, Mick. Last thing I remember is them toilets in the Old Bell.

MICK. But you remember the church, like?

DAWN. 'Course I remember the church – I ain't on about the church!

MICK. That's all I'm saying, like – everybody remembers their wedding-day.

DAWN. It's the rest of it I don't remember.

MICK. I remember us standing around outside the church, waiting for the pubs to open. Big Eddie an' all the boys, hanging around.

LEN. We went round to Jean's, didn't we?

DAWN. 'Course we did, 'course we did!

MICK. Ah yeah, you're right, man – we went round to Jean's.

DAWN. Yeah.

LEN. You laid on a right good spread, as I remember, Jean.

DAWN. She did.

LEN. Sandwiches, didn't you?

DAWN. Champagne, 'er laid on for us.

JEAN (getting up). Well, it was alright, y'know. Bridged the gap, any road.

JEAN goes into the kitchen to check the soup, and having done so, stays in the kitchen listening.

MICK. Wouldn't mind one of them sandwiches now.

DAWN. Ooh, blimey, Mick. Need a bleedin' man-'ole cover, you do.

LEN. 'T's 'ard to imagine now, intit?

DAWN. Eh?

LEN. Where was that room you 'ad, then, Jean?

DAWN. Smyrna?

LEN. Smyrna.

DAWN. Yeah.

MICK. Aw, Jes' – d'you remember us all standing round at

Smyrna? Aw, the room was smaller than this. All hunched up like sardines.

DAWN. Ah, it was lovely, though.

MICK. Aw, 'twas very nice, I'm not saying, Jean – it was very nice.

JEAN *returns, pours herself another drink, turns over the record, and sits down, whilst –*

LEN. Aye. Aye.

MICK. Then, all down the boozer soon as it opened, for a few pints.

DAWN. That was my mistake, that was.

MICK. You had to go to the pub, like. You had to put in an appearance.

DAWN. I know, but I went mad, Mick, I drunk meself stupid.

MICK. Ah well, like, you can't take it, like.

DAWN. Couldn't then, proper laid up.

LEN. Was you?

DAWN. I was – I couldn't get off me knees in them toilets. Couldn't lift me 'ead up.

MICK. I don't remember that.

DAWN. No, well you was pissed up an' all, worn't ya?

MICK. I was not pissed up, I was havin' a few jars on my wedding-day, like.

LEN. Then Jean 'ad to take you 'ome, didn't she?

JEAN. Yeah.

DAWN. She did, I was proper poorly, Len. Woke up in that room, Len, didn't know where I was. 'E worn't there, me own 'usband on me wedding-day.

MICK. I had one or two other calls to pay. Fellows wanting to shake my hands and buy me a drink – 'tis not every day you get married.

DAWN. 'Uh – start off as you mean to go on!

LEN. I was round there the other day.

DAWN. Where?

LEN. Messina.

DAWN. You worn't!

LEN. Aye, I was up that way, and I saw the 'ouse, and I
wondered if you'd still be living there – I didn't think you
would be, but I thought you might've left your address, like.

MICK. Haven't been round there this years, like.

LEN. No, no. I tapped on the window like we used to; black man
came to the door.

DAWN. Oh, blacky living there, is there?

LEN. Yeah, big, 'e was, just in 'is trousers and vest – didn't seem
to know anything about you.

DAWN. 'E wouldn't.

Pause.

LEN. We had some good times round there, though, didn't we?

MICK. Uh . . . some great nights in Messina.

LEN. Few drinks, eh?

MICK. Round there with the carry-out.

LEN. Aye. 'Course, you two were there, weren't you? Then you
moved out, and 'e moved in.

JEAN. That's right.

DAWN. Don't talk to me about Messina Avenue, Len; brought
my first babby into the world in Messina Avenue, I did.

MICK. Tracy Dawn.

DAWN. Ooh, terrible.

LEN. You 'ad 'er there, did you?

DAWN. Ooh, no. I didn't 'ave 'er there, 'ad 'er up St Mary's,
Paddington – where 'er 'ad 'ers, Princess Anne.

MICK. For Jesus' sake!

LEN. Oh? Oh, did you?

DAWN. We was livin' there, though, Len: one room.

MICK. We weren't there all that long, like.

DAWN. Long enough, Mick.

LEN. Must've been about six years ago, that, now, mustn't it?

DAWN. No.

LEN. Aye, six years.

DAWN. No, 'er's nearly eight, Tracy.

LEN. Eight?

DAWN. Yeah: 26th of January, 1972, 'er was born.

LEN. Eight years ago, is it? Doesn't seem like it, does it?

MICK. Time flies.

LEN. It does, mate, dunt it?

JEAN. You workin' tomorrow, then, Len?

LEN. No, no; the job I'm on, er, buildin' this synagogue up in 'Endon, so I don't work Saturdays.

JEAN. Oh.

MICK. Oh, yeah, the Jew-Boys, they have their Sunday on a Saturday.

LEN. Aye. Aye, that's right.

MICK. Is that a big job, Len?

LEN. No, no. It's not the synagogue itself, like, it's more like a church hall, an extension on the back, I should think it'd be about five weeks – six weeks at the most I should think, Mick.

MICK. You'll pick up another job at the end of that, no bother.

LEN. No trouble at all, no.

MICK. See, that's the way with us, Jean: we are not skilled men, but we're all-round men, like.

JEAN. Yeah.

MICK. We can walk onto the site there, we can say to the Ganger-Man, 'We can lay your cables, lay your pipes, we can do your tarmac, we can do your pavements, do your kerbs, do your concreting, di-da-di-da-di-da, like'.

LEN. You see, we're not skilled men, Jean, but we're experienced men.

JEAN. Yeah.

MICK. We work in shit. All weathers.

DAWN. Aooh, ah!!

LEN. See, that's why I come down to London, Jean; no end of building jobs going on down 'ere. Whereas, in other parts of the country – up north, for instance, not so much.

JEAN. No.

LEN. But down 'ere, as I say, if you're an experienced man, like Mick and myself, they're crying out for you – crying out.

MICK. Oh, yeah.

DAWN. Crying out for you this morning, worn't they, Mick?

MICK. They can cry out all they want: there's a bollocks up in that job, Len, I love to see him suffer.

DAWN. Proper poorly, worn't ya?

MICK. I was! I wasn't well, you know I wasn't!

LEN. D'you 'ave yer chest, did you?

MICK. Chest was at me, Len. Why would I go out on a morning like that with this chest? I'm not a fuckin' machine, like.

DAWN. The chest 'e gets of a Friday morning after being paid the Thursday night, you know what I mean, Len?

MICK. Oh, you know all about it, like – you don't have to suffer it.

DAWN. Oh, I suffer it.

MICK *has another asthma attack.*

DAWN. Want me to thump ya?

MICK. I'm alright.

DAWN. Bleedin' thump ya.

Pause.

Use too much of that spray, you do, Mick.

MICK. It's the only thing is any good for it. Don't suppose that old soup's ready, Jean?

JEAN. Will be in a minute.

DAWN. Poison, that spray is, you know, Jean. Uses too much of it. Gives 'im the shakes.

JEAN. Yeah.

Pause.

MICK. Why would I go out every day, Len? I can get the money when I want it.

DAWN. Shame it don't come my way.

MICK. What're you talkin' about? We went to Cork in the summer: hundred smackers in her hand.

DAWN. Still in me 'and when I come 'ome, Len.

MICK. That's not what I'm saying: you got the money.

LEN. Mick was telling me about your 'oliday in Cork, Dawn. Sounds as if you 'ad a nice time?

MICK. We'd a lovely time, Len.

DAWN. Punishment, Len: punishment.

MICK. What are you talking about?

DAWN. What's the use of a 'undred pound, Mick, when there's nowhere to bleedin' spend it?

MICK. Well, the kiddies had a lovely time to themselves.

DAWN. They was over-excited.

MICK. They were excited because they'd never been by the seaside before.

DAWN. They was excited because they couldn't get out the bleedin' caravan, raining all the time.

MICK. My arse.

DAWN. Nothing for 'em to do, Len: bored stiff, they was.

MICK (*undertone*). Thanks very much.

DAWN.   (*undertone*). 'D'you mean?

JEAN.   } This is Dolly Parton, Len. (*She is referring to the record.*)

LEN. Aye, aye. She's good, int she? Me wife used to 'ave a few of 'ers.

MICK. Who's that?

JEAN. Dolly Parton.

MICK. Oh – very good.

LEN. She's got a nice personality, ant she?

JEAN. Yeah.

MICK. Nice voice, an' all.

JEAN. Yeah.

DAWN. Looks like a bleedin' man dressed up as a woman, 'er.

MICK. I'm sorry, Dawn; like, I beg your pardon, I'm sorry to contradict you here, like, but how can she look like a man when she's got diddies out to here?

DAWN. Well, Danny La Bleedin' Rue's got diddies out to there – you'd fancy 'im, you.

MICK. I'm not talking about Danny La Bleeding Rue, I'm talking about Dolly Parton, and she doesn't look like a man.

DAWN. 'Er ain't natural. Put a bit of Elvis on, Jean.

JEAN. Yeah.

LEN. Oh, you got Elvis, 'ave you?

JEAN. Yeah.

DAWN. Yeah, we bought it for 'er for 'er birthday.

JEAN. 'T's good.

DAWN. Yeah – 'Greatest 'Its'.

LEN. Shame about 'im dying, wasn't it?

JEAN. Yeah.

DAWN. Ooh – I loved 'im Elvis, I did – loved 'im.

JEAN. And me.

MICK. Funny the way they all die, those stars. You got Elvis . . . Jim Reeves.

LEN. Jim Reeves.

MICK. Buddy Holly.

JEAN. Mind you, they were killed, weren't they?

MICK. They were killed.

JEAN. Buddy 'Olly, 'e was only 26, y'know. 'S young, that, init?

LEN. Oh, aye.

DAWN. Ah, but 'e got too fat, though, Elvis: see the state of 'im
    before 'e died, Jean?

JEAN. It's the drugs, weren'it? Blew 'im up?

DAWN. I don't know, you know.

JEAN. Ooh, it was.

MICK. You would never've taken Elvis for a junkie.

DAWN. You wouldn't; 'e worn't no long-'air, Elvis.

LEN. 'E was ill, wa'n't 'e?

DAWN. 'E was, you know.

LEN. They wouldn't 'ave given 'im all them drugs if 'e 'ant been
    ill.

DAWN. 'Course they wouldn't. You know what I think, Len? I
    don't reckon 'e knowed about them drugs.

LEN. No.

JEAN. 'Course he knew about 'em – 'e'd got 'yperdermic needles
    and boxes of pills all over the place at 'ome.

DAWN. No – them was doctors' drugs, Jean!

JEAN. No, 'e was bribing the doctors to give 'im all them.

LEN. Oh, aye, but 'e didn't smoke pot and that, did 'e?

JEAN. Oh no, no – 'e'd left that be'ind a long time ago.

LEN. Ah, well, there y'are, you see, that's what I'm saying, 'e
    wasn't like the Rolling Stones and them, was 'e?

MICK. Oh, no, Elvis was more clean-livin' than what the Rolling
    Stones were.

LEN.   ⎫   Aye.
DAWN. ⎭   Ooh ah.

JEAN. Ah, well, they've all got too much money anyway, int they? They don't know what to do with it.

DAWN. Oh ah, it's money kills 'em, Jean.

MICK. Ah, this is it: they can't take the strain. Like meself.

LEN. I know what you mean, Mick, I know what you mean – I don't know what to do with all my money.

DAWN. Don't you, Len?

LEN. I thought I might buy a yacht, or I might . . .

Short pause.

JEAN. I wouldn't like a lot of money, me.

LEN. Wouldn't you?

JEAN. Well, not that much, any road. You go and die and leave it, don't you?

LEN. Aye, you can't take it with you, can you?

JEAN. You can't.

MICK. You can hit it a bit of a kick before you go.

JEAN. } Mm.
DAWN. } Mm.

Pause.

MICK. What'd you do now, Len, if you had a million pounds?

LEN. } Ooh!
JEAN. } Oh!
DAWN. } Ooh, blimey!

DAWN. Tell you what I'd do.

JEAN. What?

DAWN. Get meself a full-time baby-minder, twenty-four hours a day.

MICK. What do you think I pay you for?

DAWN. I wouldn't need your twenty quid, would I, if I 'ad a million pounds.

LEN. I think I'd get meself a little boat, down by the sea, do a bit of fishing.

JEAN. You like fishing, don't you, Len?

LEN. I do, I do.

Pause.

What'd you do, then, Jean?

JEAN. Me? I'd go to America.

LEN. Would you?

JEAN. I'd love it.

LEN. You always wanted to do a bit of travelling, didn't you?

JEAN. Yeah, go abroad.

LEN. D'you ever go?

JEAN. No.

LEN. Didn't you?

JEAN. No.

LEN. Aah.

MICK. I have a sister in Chicago.

JEAN.   } Mm.
LEN.   } Oh?

DAWN. Ar, 'e 'as.

Pause.

LEN. What'd you do, then, Mick?

MICK. If I had a million pounds?

LEN. Aye.

MICK. I'd buy meself a pub.

DAWN. 'E would, 'n all, 'im.

MICK. I wouldn't bother opening it. I'd just sit in it meself.

JEAN. Well, you got a ready-maid barmaid anyway, ent ya?

DAWN. Blimey, Jean, you'd never be off your bleedin' feet, servin' 'im.

MICK. Don't worry yourself – big sign over the door: MEN ONLY, SELF-SERVICE.

DAWN. You could see it, couldn't you? Parlatic from morning till night.

MICK. And why the fuck not? Come on, this is supposed to be a party – come on, drink up there.

LEN. Right. Lager, Dawn?

DAWN. Yes, please, Len, lovely.

MICK. Your vodka is sittin' there.

DAWN. Ooh, don't want no vodka, Mick. Alright, go on, go on, go on, crack it open.

LEN. Don't you want a lager?

DAWN. Aye, I'll 'ave a lager an 'all.

LEN. Right.

> JEAN *puts the soup on the table.*

MICK. There's my lovely soup coming.

DAWN. Lovely.

LEN. Spot of tonic in it, Dawn?

DAWN. Aye, throw it in there, Len.

MICK. Tell you what, Len-Baby, I'll sit there to take the ole loop-de-loop.

LEN. Eh? Oh, sorry Mick.

> MICK *and* LEN *change places.*

LEN. Right mate? Right. Smells good, that soup.

JEAN. There's some bread 'ere.

DAWN. 'Ungry, am you, Len?

LEN. No, I 'ad my tea before I came out.

DAWN. Did ya?

LEN. Oh, yes.

DAWN. Yeah.

> JEAN *has sat down.*

LEN. Sorry, Jean, I didn't get you yours – d'you want some gin, Jean?

DAWN (*taking cigarette*). Oh ah. Alright, am yer, Jean?

JEAN. Yeah, yeah.

DAWN. 'T's alright like this, the bed, enit?

JEAN. Oh ah, yeah, lovely. Er, cigarette, Len?

LEN. No, I've got one on, thank you, Jean.

MICK. This out of a tin, Jean?

JEAN. Oh, ah.

MICK. She always gets me it out of a packet, like, but this is very nice.

LEN. 'Ere y'are, Jean.

JEAN (*taking drink*). Thanks, Len.

DAWN. Alright am yer, Len?

LEN. Aye.

DAWN. Goin' to stay down 'ere now, am yer?

LEN. I might do; see 'ow it goes, like.

JEAN. See if you like it, eh?

LEN. Aye. If I like it, I might get meself sorted out and stop down 'ere, otherwise I might . . . go somewhere else.

DAWN. You don't miss 'er, do ya?

MICK. Ar, for Jesus' sake, give the man peace – you're like a dog with a bone. Pay no attention to her, Len – 'tis like goin' to fuckin' confession with her.

LEN. Aye, alright.

DAWN. You want to enjoy yourself, you do, Len. 'E's been through it, 'e 'as.

MICK. Well, if he didn't go through it before, he's going through it now!

DAWN. Looks well though, don't 'e, Jean?

JEAN. Yeah.

MICK. Looks fuckin' great.

LEN. Open air life – nothing like it.

DAWN. No 'e looks very well.

JEAN. I like you in them glasses, Len.

LEN. Huh . . . hide my face, don't they?

JEAN. No . . .

MICK. Hide the ugly old mug!

JEAN. No, I mean – they suit you.

LEN. Oh . . . cheers, anyway.

DAWN. ⎫ Cheers!

JEAN. ⎭ Cheers!

MICK. All the very best.

JEAN. 'Ave you done any fishing since you've been down 'ere, Len?

LEN. No, no, I left me rods up at me mother's like. If I decide to stop down 'ere, I daresay I'll go and pick 'em up, like.

DAWN. D'you eat them fish what you catch, do you, Len?

LEN. Some of them, aye. Some of the seafish make good eating.

DAWN. Do you?

LEN. Mm.

DAWN. Blimey.

JEAN. Lovely.

DAWN. Give us a taste o' that soup, Mick.

MICK. I will in my bollocks.

DAWN. Go on, I only want a taste.

MICK. This is my dinner. You had your dinner. Keep your nose out of my soup.

DAWN. Mean-'earted, you am.

MICK. Kiss my face.

DAWN. I'm goin' on the toilet, Jean.

JEAN. Alright.

> DAWN *has gone*.

> *Pause.*

JEAN. So d'you still get them 'eadaches, then, Len?

LEN. No, no, no I don't. The glasses seem to 'ave done the trick, aye.

JEAN. Ah, so it must've been starin' at the water strained your eyes.

LEN. Aye, watching the float, like, you see.

JEAN. Oh.

LEN. Anyway, as I say, I 'aven't 'ad a recurrence since I got 'em, so I put it down to that, aye.

JEAN. Good.

LEN. Ridiculous really, intit, goin' out for a day's fishing, and coming back with a 'eadache?

JEAN. Yeah – supposed to be enjoying yourself, ent ya?

LEN. Aye.

MICK. Thanks be to God I have no trouble with me eyes.

LEN. Aye, you're a lucky man there, Mick.

MICK. Ah well, we all have our little faults.

LEN. Aye.

MICK. You got your glasses; I got my chest; Dawn has her old mouth.

LEN. Ah, she's a good girl, Mick – you look after 'er.

> *Pause.*

> What's that you're reading there, then, Jean?

JEAN. This? That's Marilyn Monroe, but I've only read bits o' that.

LEN. Oh. Like 'er life-story, is it?

JEAN. Yeah, well – you know me: I always liked reading biographies.

LEN. Oh, aye, that's right, I remember, aye. I like novels meself. Harold Robbins, 'e's one of my favourites.

JEAN. Oh, yeah?

LEN. Ever read any of 'im?

JEAN. No.

LEN. Aye, very good stories, 'e writes. *Carpetbaggers* – that's one of 'is.

JEAN. Oh, I've read that.

LEN. That's it.

JEAN. Oh?

LEN. 'T's good, intit?

JEAN. Yeah.

MICK. Well, that was a fine drop of soup, Jean. Oh, that hit the spot.

JEAN. That's good.

MICK. I feel like a new man now. Jes's, I'm ready for a session now. Come on, Hardwick: drink up. I never saw you so slow.

LEN. Oh, don't you worry about me, mate – I'll keep up wi' you.

MICK. Jean – what about you?

JEAN. Oh, I'm alright, 'ere, Mick, thanks.

LEN. Jean, Jean, if you want to get to bed, like, just turn us out – don't let us overstay our welcome, like.

JEAN. No, don't be so silly.

MICK. Oh, for Jesus' sake, d'you know who you're talking to? This is Jean! This girl is a stayer – she'll drink us all under the table in no time. I'll say that for you, Jean: you could always take a drink. Oh, yeah, I've seen you in some sessions, hey? Drinkin' and singin' away to the small hours. D'you ever know about this girl, Len? – Lovely singer.

LEN. Oh, I'd forgotten that, Jean.

MICK. Aye, lovely voice –

LEN. – I remember, aye –

MICK. – Very sweet voice –

LEN. – Aye.

MICK. Oh, yeah. I love to hear her singin'. Tell you what, Jean.

JEAN. What?

MICK. I'll have one of your old songs off you before I go.

JEAN. Ooh, I dunno.

LEN. Aye, you'll 'ave to give us one, Jean.

MICK. Aye, yeah, Jean, lovely singer, ah yeah, you will – give us a song before I go.

JEAN. Can't remember 'em now.

MICK. Ar, Jean, pull the other one, 't 'as bells on. Go on, you'll give us one, won't you?

JEAN. I'll 'ave to 'ave another bottle o' gin first.

MICK. There's no problems with the old gin, Jean. Huh. Am I right?

LEN. Aye.

DAWN *returns.*

MICK. Am n' I right?

DAWN. 'Speak to me!

MICK. Ar, come near me.

MICK *draws* DAWN *to him, and she sits on his lap.*

DAWN. You've been mean to me, you 'ave.

MICK. Ar, give us an ole smile, it's supposed to be a party. I'm only sayin' to Jean here, we'll have a song off her before we go.

DAWN. Ar, only if 'er wants to.

MICK. Oh, I wouldn't twist her arm, like.

LEN. No no.

MICK (*to* DAWN). Come on, you! Drink up – enjoy yourself.

DAWN. ⎫ Cheers!

LEN.   ⎬ Cheers!

JEAN. ⎭ Cheers!

MICK. All the Hairy Breast!

DAWN. 'Be rude!

MICK. Jean –

JEAN. Yeah?

MICK. It's very nice for me to be takin' a drink in your house.

JEAN. Ooh yeah, yeah.

MICK. Like, I only live around the corner, but we sort o' way lost touch, yourself and meself, over the last little while.

JEAN. Yeah.

MICK. And I'm sorry for it, and we won't let it be so long again.

JEAN. No, we wunt.

MICK. Okay.

JEAN. Yeah.

MICK. And, Jean –

JEAN. Yeah?

MICK. I'll have an ole song off you before I go.

JEAN. Oh!

DAWN. Cheers!

LEN. Cheers!

JEAN. Cheers!

DAWN. 'Ey, Jean, 'ave a bit of Elvis on.

LEN. Aye.

DAWN. Ain't 'ad 'im on yet.

JEAN. Let's 'ave a bit of 'im on.

(*She starts putting on the record: Elvis Presley,* 40 Greatest Hits, *Record One, side one, 'My Baby Left Me'.*)

MICK. We'll have Elvis first, and then we'll have Jean.

JEAN. Then we'll show 'im up, eh?

MICK. Aw, Jesus, I had some drinks today.

DAWN. Ooh, blimey, you don't say.

MICK. I'm worn out picking winners.

LEN. Aye, you 'ad a lucky day, didn't you?

MICK. Yeah, I picked myself a nice little winner at Lingfield.
Then I met Sullivan, and I took some money off him at the
cards.

DAWN. 'Ow much d'you win off 'im?

MICK. Enough, like. I didn't take it all off him – I didn't want to
leave him short, like, you know.

DAWN. I never win nothing, I don't.

MICK. Ah, well, don't worry yourself, you've got a good-looking
husband.

DAWN. Ooh blimey, 'ark at 'im!

The music starts.

MICK. Elvis. The King.

JEAN. Yeah.

MICK. D'you ever go to an ole dance at all, Len?

LEN. Oh, we used to go a bit – occasionally, like.

DAWN. 'E does, don't ya?

MICK. Oh yes, I still go up to the 'National'.

LEN. Aye?

MICK. Or the 'Galtimore'.

LEN. Oh aye.

MICK. Dance all the way to the bar.

DAWN. Ooh ah.

MICK. She won't come with me.

DAWN. I bleedin' wunt – not after the last time I went wi' ya.

MICK. Oh, that's the way with me – dance all the way to the bar, like. Then dance all the way to the toilet. Then dance all the way back to the bar.

LEN. Aye. Aye. Know what you mean, mate.

JEAN. I ain't been to a dance for ages.

LEN. No, I an't, Jean.

DAWN. Ain't ya, Len?

LEN. No, we used to go a bit on 'oliday, like, at Skeg', but that'd be more discos, that's for the kids really, intit?

JEAN. Makes you feel old, dunnit, Len?

LEN. It does, dunt it?

MICK. I could never be bothered with a disco; I'd rather have a live band – like a show band.

LEN. Aye. Aye.

JEAN. We used to go a lot, dint we?

DAWN. Ooh, we did. We used to dance together, me'n 'er.

LEN. Did you?

JEAN. Ooh, ah, I loved it.

DAWN. Ooh, I did, Jean.

LEN. What they do that for, then?

DAWN. Eh? – Safer, Len.

JEAN. Ooh, ah! – What's safe about it?

DAWN. Ooh ah, I know, you could get some rough buggers down them places, you could see 'em coming across the floor towards you, and you knew.

JEAN. Ah, well, that's what we used to do it for, init?

DAWN. Ooh, ah – cattle market.

MICK *makes cattle noises.*

Eh? Ooh, don't be silly. I used to get dead sick, though, I did, Jean: always got the bleedin' ugly ones.

MICK. Thanks very much.

DAWN. Oh, no, it was different wi' you, Mick – took pity on you!
No, we used to love the dancing, didn't we, Jean?

JEAN. Ooh, ah.

DAWN. We used to dance up the caff. Remember? The Coppola
Arch?

JEAN. Coppola Arch!

DAWN. We used to be on them bleedin' tables, some nights.

JEAN. And that was just on a Coca-Cola.

DAWN. Oh, we didn't need no drink in them days, Len. D'you
remember Kevin?

JEAN. Ooh, ah.

DAWN. 'E was a good dancer, worn'e? Bought me eternity ring,
'e did.

JEAN. Ooh, ah, I remember that.

DAWN. Yeah. Could be a cunt, though.

*LEN starts to join in quietly with Elvis, tapping his foot to the music.
Then MICK joins in, also quietly. The girls carry on over this, not
noticing it yet.*

DAWN. 'Ey, what wa that little un's name, Jean?

JEAN. Which one?

DAWN. You know . . . 'e was only little, only 'ad a little bike,
never 'ad a girlfriend, used to dance with a chair?

JEAN. Colin.

DAWN. Colin!

JEAN. Colin and Jeff – they were two brothers, Colin and Jeff. I
used to dance with 'im sometimes.

DAWN. Ah – you was doin' 'im a favour though, worn't ya?

JEAN. Well, I felt sorry for 'im.

DAWN (*indicating the boys*). Jean!

JEAN. Yeah.

LEN/MICK. 'Since my baby left me,
I found a new place to dwell

Down at the bottom of Lonely Street,
The Heartbreak Hotel.
I'm feeling so lonely,
I'm feeling so lonely, baby,
I'm feeling so lonely,
I could die . . .'

DAWN. Len.

LEN. Yeah?

DAWN. 'Tain't upsetting you, is it?

LEN. No, no, don't worry about me!

DAWN. Know you can feel free, don't ya – you'm among friends, don't you 'old it in.

MICK. Ah, footloose and fancy free.

DAWN. Ah, but a sad song, see? Can upset a person.

MICK (*loudly, and imitating Elvis*). 'Since ma baby left me . . .' (*etc.*)

JEAN. Ooh, en 'e good?

> MICK *continues imitation.*

JEAN. Sounds just like 'im, dunt 'e?

LEN. Aye, dunt 'e?

MICK. Oh, I could always do Elvis. You know.

DAWN. Jean! Jean: two of us on the backs o' them bikes!

JEAN. I know. It was dangerous, really, wunnit?

DAWN. Ooh!

JEAN. 'Cos we dain't wear no 'elmets, you know, 'cos you din' 'ave to, then . . .

LEN. No, you wouldn't . . .

JEAN. – It was just our bare 'eads.

DAWN. Remember that accident?

JEAN. Tommy!

DAWN. Ooh – on the way to Stourport, come off.

JEAN. Wa'n' 'e a mess, ey?

DAWN. Broke 'is arm.

MICK. We've seen some accidents. Eh, Len?

LEN. Ah.

JEAN. 'Ey: what about the day they all got picked up?

DAWN. The lads? Ooh, ah. 'Er went up the bleedin' Police
    Station, 'er did – layin' down the law to the coppers, 'er was!

JEAN. Nearly got meself put inside!

MICK. Pair of criminals, these two, Len!

LEN. Aye, Jean, Jean: wasn't it you 'oo told me about –

JEAN. Yeah, yeah – this is it –

LEN. – Mods and Rockers?

JEAN. – Yeah . . .

DAWN. Margate!

LEN. Oh.

JEAN. There was a great big fight, see, an' they all got arrested.

LEN. Oh, aye?

MICK. Pair o' Rockers, these two, Len.

JEAN. Oh, ah: we used to do ton-ups down the M1 'an't we?

DAWN. Yeah – silly, Jean!

    Pause.

JEAN. D'you remember that really bad fight with Tommy and
    . . . er . . . Den?

    Short pause.

DAWN. No.

JEAN. No – it was Colin.

DAWN. Ooh ah – wi' knives!

JEAN. 'E just touched Den's bike, an' 'e din' 'alf lay into 'im, din'
    'e?

DAWN. Abergelly.

JEAN. That's it!

MICK. We've seen some fights, eh, Len?

LEN. Oh, aye. Were they older than you, these boys, then, Jean?

JEAN. } Ooh, ah.

DAWN. } Ooh, ah – we was only kids, Len.

Pause.

JEAN. You used to 'ave a bike, din' you, Len?

LEN. Ah, when I was a lad, like, aye.

DAWN. Was yer a leather boy, was yer, Len?

LEN. For a year or so, like, aye.

JEAN. What was it?

LEN. A B.S.A.

JEAN. Oh, a Beezer. We didn't 'ave any o' them, did we?

DAWN. No.

LEN. No, this was an old bike – ten or fifteen year old when I 'ad it.

JEAN. They were all Nortons and Triumphs, wun' they?

DAWN. Yeah – Bonnyvilles.

LEN. Oh, no, no, no – I wasn't part of a gang, like.

DAWN. You 'ave a little girlfriend for the back, did ya?

LEN. From time to time, like. I got rid of it though.

DAWN. Did ya? Why?

LEN. I couldn't stand the cold, to be quite frank with you.

DAWN. Ooh!

JEAN. Bitter, wa'n' it?

DAWN. Ooh, could be very chilly – I used to get that cystitis, I did – on the toilet all the time, stinging, y'know.

MICK. How did you get that?

DAWN. Wind blowin' up yer skirt.

MICK. Oh-Ooh!

He puts his hand up DAWN's skirt.

DAWN (*laughing*). 'Ey – 'be rude!

JEAN. I bet we didn't 'alf look a sight, ey, on the backs of them bikes in them short skirts!

LEN. Mini-skirts.

MICK. I don't know, now, Len – I think the pair o'them have got very nice sets o'legs.

LEN. Oh, aye, aye, they 'ave, aye.

MICK. Jes', I don't know, this one has got shins so sharp you could shear a hedge with them.

DAWN. 'Be rude.

MICK. I'm only joking.

DAWN. Always goin' on about my body, you am.

MICK. You can't take a joke.

DAWN. Can.

MICK. Think you've got a very nice body. Kept your figure well. Jean – she's kept herself in trim, like.

JEAN. Yeah, yeah.

MICK. Know what I mean, Len like? Even though I do say it myself. She doesn't look like the mother of three kiddies.

JEAN *gets up, quickly and unobtrusively, pours herself a drink, and then stays up and at the drinks, facing away from the others.*

LEN (*continuing directly*). No, no: you've kept yourself very well, Dawn, no doubt about it.

MICK. That's what I'm saying, like. Oh, Lord Jesus, some of the ones, you see them on the Kilburn High Road, they have let themselves go, like; three or four kiddies in the pram, piled high with shopping bags, aw, Lord Jes', 'twould turn your stomach.

LEN. Aye.

MICK. Some of them are twenty-five, and they look forty-five, all fat and flabby, holes in their stockings. 'Twould make you wonder what they think of themselves.

LEN. Aye.

MICK. And their blokes, like. Some of the young ones, like, I see
   them when I'm up at the Dance, seventeen or eighteen years
   old, they got all the latest fashions, showing off their bodies,
   throwing themselves around the floor, making up to the
   geezers.

LEN. Aye.

MICK. But what are they? They're fuck all!

LEN. Aye.

MICK. There's nothing to them, Jean, you know.

JEAN. Mm.

MICK. But this one . . . this one is different.

LEN. Mm.

MICK. Dawn is a woman.

LEN. Aye.

DAWN. Eh?

MICK. Well, like, there's more to you than that, like.

DAWN. Oh.

MICK. I mean it now, I'm not bullshitt'n'. If you came up to the
   Dance with me, you'd show some of them young ones up.

DAWN. 'Be silly.

MICK. Jes', I don't know why you wouldn't bother coming up
   with me, like.

DAWN. You know.

MICK. Come up and give me an ole dance now and again.

DAWN. Goin' no Dances wi' you.

MICK. Come on, gimme a dance now.

   He picks her up, and throws her about.

DAWN (*basically amused*). Don't be silly!

MICK. Oh, yeah!

DAWN. No, Mick!

MICK. Come on!

DAWN. No! Oh, geroff!

MICK. Hey, hey!

DAWN. Don't, you'll throw me back out.

MICK. Come on now!

DAWN. Careful, you'll have me throwing up.

> MICK *puts* DAWN *down.* JEAN *sits.*

LEN. I thought 'e were going to drop you then, Dawn.

DAWN. I know – 'e would, an' all, 'im. Rough bugger.

> *Pause: Elvis has begun, 'Love Me Tender'. The pause continues:*
> MICK *and* DAWN *cuddle up, then a few affectionate kisses, then a*
> *prolonged kiss. Then, quietly . . .*

DAWN. Let's 'ave a dance.

MICK. Oh, all of a sudden you want to dance.

DAWN. Oh, this is different.

MICK. I'm half-cut.

DAWN. I know, I am, an' all. Come on – don't matter.

> MICK *and* DAWN *get up and dance.*

> *After a short time,* MICK *taps* LEN *with his foot, and winks,*
> *gesturing him to dance with* JEAN.

> JEAN *immediately gets up and leaves the room.*

> *Pause. Elvis continues.* MICK *and* DAWN *continue to dance. Then*
> . . .

DAWN. Lovely to see you together, Len. You was fond of 'er,
worn't yer?

LEN. Oh, we always got on well, me an' Jean, aye.

DAWN. Get 'er to 'ave a dance wi' you, Len.

LEN. No . . .

MICK. Ar, go on, man – have a dance.

> LEN *laughs.*

> *As the track ends,* MICK *and* DAWN *have a prolonged kiss.*

> *The next track starts, 'Got A Lot of Livin' To Do', and* MICK *thrusts*
> DAWN *into a fast jive.*

MICK. Oh, that's more like it!

DAWN. No! I don't wanna do no rough dancing!

MICK. That's the kind I like.

They fall on the bed.

MICK. How did that happen?

DAWN. Aargh! Don't start gerrin' sexy! – 'Ey!

JEAN returns.

DAWN. Alright, am ya, Jean?

JEAN. Yeah, Yeah. 'Ow's everybody's glasses? Alright?

LEN. Aye, aye – come on!

MICK. Oh, I wouldn't mind an old jar.

JEAN. Len.

LEN. D'you want some tonic in that, Dawn?

DAWN. Ooh, ah.

JEAN. Mick.

MICK. Thanks very much, Jean.

LEN. 'Ere y'are.

MICK. I'll 'ave a drop of that vodka.

DAWN. You'll be sick, you will, Mick.

LEN. Want some tonic in there, Jean?

JEAN. Yes please, Len.

LEN. Say when.

JEAN. Right, that's lovely, thanks – don't wanna drown it.

LEN. No. (*Offering a cigarette.*) 'Ere y'are, Jean.

JEAN. Thanks, Len.

LEN. Dawn?

MICK. Here, I'll light that for her.

DAWN. Don't you inhale it, Mick.

MICK. No problems.

DAWN. You dare!

LEN. Dunt look right you with a fag in your mouth, mate.

DAWN. It don't.

LEN. Jean.

JEAN. I done it, Len, thanks.

LEN. Oh, aye – you're alright.

MICK. Come on, Jean – get the old record out of the way, and let's have a proper singsong.

JEAN. } Oh, ah. That sounds more like it.

LEN. } Oh, aye, let's 'ave a singsong, aye.

MICK (*withholding* DAWN's *cigarette*). What do I get for it?

DAWN. Oh, ah.

> DAWN *kisses* MICK. *He gives her the cigarette. He gets up.* JEAN *is seeing to the record.*

JEAN. Right . . .

MICK. Aw, here, I have to go to the toilet.

JEAN. Oh.

MICK. I have a loaded weapon. Jean, don't start without me.

JEAN. No – can't start without you; you know all the songs.

> DAWN *is also crossing the room.*

LEN. Are you going with 'im, Dawn?

DAWN. No – goin' to gerra drink o' water.

JEAN. There's a cup up there.

DAWN (*from kitchen*). Oh ar, I gorrit, Jean.

LEN. 'Ow much d'you pay for this room, if you don't mind me asking, Jean?

JEAN. Nineteen a week.

LEN. Nineteen pounds a week?

DAWN. Terrible, init, Len?

JEAN. Expensive, init? Eh?

LEN. Shocking.

JEAN. You thinkin' of moving out of your digs, then, Len?

LEN. Well, if I decide to stop down 'ere I'm thinking I might, but . . . nineteen pounds a week! Terrible price to pay!

JEAN. Well, that's 'ow much they cost now, see? 'Cos of course there int many about, so they just charge what they like.

LEN. Oh. But that other place you 'ad, er –

JEAN. Smyrna Road?

LEN. Smyrna Road, 'ow much was that?

JEAN. Oh, that was only eight.

LEN. Eight?

JEAN. But of course, that was a few years ago now.

LEN. Oh, aye, but eight to nineteen, that's er, that's – oo – that's over a 'undred per cent inflation – rocketing inflation, that is.

DAWN. Mmm.

JEAN. Well, you ain't gonna get anywhere like Messina Avenue, I mean that was only a fiver – well, it was four pounds, nineteen and six.

DAWN (*in unison*). – nineteen and six. For the two of us, mind, Len. Only one bed, though, Jean.

JEAN. Oh, ah, but it was still only one room, wunnit?

DAWN. Ah. (*Pause.*) Did 'er keep you waitin' again today, that woman?

JEAN. } Ooh, bloody 'ell!
DAWN. } Did 'er?

JEAN. Yeah. See, Len, the bloke 'oo owns these 'ouses, 'e owns a dress-shop on the 'Igh Road, see? An' I 'ave to go up there after work of a Friday, pay the rent.

DAWN. 'T's 'is wife, enit, Jean?

JEAN. Yeah. D'you know, I got in there today, an 'er'd got a girl in the back room, 'er was givin' 'er a fittin' for a wedding dress, so of course I was 'anging about for about twenty minutes.

LEN. No.

JEAN. I 'ave to wait, see, Len, 'cos 'er 'as to check me money and then write it in the rent-book, see?

LEN. No, no.

DAWN. Bleedin' cheek, enit, Len?

LEN. Terrible, ent it?

DAWN. Treat you like muck.

MICK *returns.*

MICK. Right, that's my throat cleared. Come on, Missus, sit down: we're going to start the singsong.

LEN. Aye, come on, let's get t'singsong going, then.

MICK. Come on, Jean – you get us kicked off.

LEN. Go on, Jean!

JEAN. Ooh, come on! You're the one that knows all the songs.

MICK. Ah, no Jean – you're the singer, come on now.

LEN. Come on, Jean!

JEAN. Ooh, I can't remember 'em now.

MICK. Aw, Dawn – what were the songs she used to sing?

DAWN. Ooh, I can't remember the names of 'em Mick?

MICK. Aw Jes' Christ, Jes', you had dozens of 'em, Jean.

JEAN (*sings*). 'Oh Danny Boy, the pipes,
                    The pipes are calling . . .'
        Come on, you all know this one.

LEN *joins in, flat, and tagging behind* JEAN.

JEAN/LEN. 'From Glen to Glen,
                    And round the mountain side.'

MICK. One voice: one singer, one song!

LEN. Sorry, mate, you're right, aye.

JEAN (*not having stopped*). 'The summer's gone,
        And all the leaves are dying.
        'Tis you, 'tis you are gone,
        And I must bide.

But come ye back
When summer's in the meadow,
Or when the valley's hushed,
And white with snow –

MICK (*harmonising*). And white with snow.

JEAN. 'Tis I'll be here
In sunshine er in shadow,
Oh, Danny Boy,
Oh, Danny Boy,
I love you so.' There y'are.

DAWN. } Oooh.
LEN. } Aaah.

MICK. Ah, Jean; from the heart: that was magic.

MICK *kisses* JEAN.

DAWN. Ooh, blimey! That's got to 'im, Jean.

MICK. Ah, that song gets me.

LEN. You've got a lovely voice, Jean.

JEAN. Ooh, gerrawf!

LEN. She's got a much better voice than some of them you get on telly, an't she?

MICK. Ar, the telly's all crap!

LEN. You ought to tek it up, Jean.

JEAN. Ooh, ah! (*To* MICK.) Come on, you do one now.

LEN. Come on, Mick.

MICK. Oh, no: I wouldn't follow that.

LEN. Ah, come on, mate.

JEAN. Len, come on: you do one!

MICK. Yeah, come on Len – your turn.

LEN. Oh, no!

DAWN. You used to know lots, you did, Len.

LEN. I only know t'dirty-uns we used to sing in the pub, like.

JEAN. Do one o'them.

MICK. Len, Len: give us one of your old Corby ones!

LEN. I don't know as I can remember 'em, er . . . oh, yeah. Er . . . Yeah . . .

> *He sings . . .*

> 'I knew a farmer, and I knew 'im well.
> I knew 'is daughter, and 'er name was Nell.
> She was so pretty, and only sixteen,
> And I showed 'er the works
> Of my threshing-machine.'

DAWN. Ooh!

> JEAN *joins in the chorus.*

LEN/JEAN. 'I 'ad 'er, I 'ad 'er, I 'ad 'er, I 'av.
> I 'ad 'er, I 'ad 'er, I showed 'er the way.
> They were the best days of my life,
> I would say,
> And I spent 'em a-leading
> Young maidens a-stray.'

LEN (*solo*). I went to the farm, I took 'er one day,
> I took 'er inside,
> An' I showed 'er the 'ay.
> And under the 'ay,
> Where we could not be seen,
> I showed 'er the works
> Of my threshing-machine.'

MICK. You dirty bollocks!

> LEN *and* JEAN *sing the chorus.* MICK *claps.*

LEN (*solo*). 'Now, three months later
> Could plainly be seen
> A bulge in 'er pinny
> Where no bulge 'ad been.
> And three months later
> Could plainly be seen
> The result of 'er playin'
> Wi' my threshing-machine.'

> LEN *and* JEAN *sing the chorus.* MICK *does the odd whoop, in the Country and Western style.*

LEN (*solo*). 'Now, three months later,
   The baby was born,
   The baby was born
   On a bright summer's morn.
   And between 'is legs
   Could plainly be seen
   A brand – new twin-cylinder
   Threshing-machine.'

DAWN. Oooh . . . dirty!

   LEN *and* JEAN *sing the chorus, then* . . .

LEN. I can't remember any more.

JEAN. Ooh, it's good, that one, Len.

DAWN. Didn't know you knew songs like that, Len. Dark 'orse, 'e is. Jean –

JEAN. Eh?

DAWN. Jean – what was tharrun?

JEAN. What?

DAWN (*sings*). 'I stood on the bridge at midnight . . .'

JEAN. Ooh, yeah – no, no, . . .
   (*Sings.*) 'It's the same the whole world over,
   It's the poor what gets the blame,
   It's the rich what gets the pleasure,
   Ain't it all a blooming shame?'

DAWN (*singing in unison*). '. . . Fucking shame?'

MICK. Hey, you, watch your language!

JEAN (*sings solo*). 'She was poor, but she was honest . . .'

   Pause.

JEAN. } Ooh!
DAWN. } Oooh, blimey . . .

   Pause.

JEAN/DAWN. 'She was poor, but she was honest . . .'

DAWN. Was about some rich geezer did it on 'er, wor'n it?

JEAN. Yeah.

MICK. Ah, Jean, give us another old Irish one, like.

JEAN. Ooh, you're the one that knows all the Irish ones.

LEN. Aye, Mick, come on.

MICK. Aw, no.

DAWN. No, 'e ain't got a note in 'is 'ead.

MICK. Fuck off! I could've sung in show bands!

JEAN. 'Ey, Len: you'd know this one. The only bit I know, is it
    goes,
    'Ta-rum, titty-bum, titty-bum, titty-bum.'

LEN/JEAN (*joining in*). 'Ta-rum, titty-bum, titty-bum, titty-bum.'

JEAN. That's the one.

> LEN *and* JEAN *continue to sing* 'Ta-rum', *etc., during which*
> DAWN *sings quietly to herself,*

DAWN. 'Roll me over,
    In the clover,
    Roll me over,
    Lay me down,
    And do it again . . .'

LEN (*to* JEAN). I know it – 'Ta-rum, titty-bum, titty-bum, titty-
    bum –'

MICK. Ah, ta-rum titty fuckin' bum!

LEN. I can't remember it, Jean, it's gone.

JEAN (*sings*). 'When I was young,
    I used to be
    As fine a lad
    As ever you'd see,
    And the Prince o' Wales,
    He said to me,
    "Come and join
    The British Army!" '

> MICK *joins in with the chorus* . . .

JEAN/MICK. 'Too-ra-loo-ra-loo-ra-loo,
    They're looking for monkies
    Up in the zoo,
    And if I had a face like you,
    I'd join the British Army!'

JEAN. That's good, init?

LEN. Oh. Come on, Jean – come on.

MICK. Don't stop now, Jean.

JEAN. Oh, I can't remember the other verses.

MICK. Oh, I love that one.

JEAN. Yeah; an' me, but they go out yer 'ead, dun't they? Come on, you do one, now.

LEN. Come on, Mick – your turn now. Come on, mate.

MICK. Ar, no, I won't bother.

LEN.   }   Oh, come on, Mick.

DAWN. }   Oh, come on!

JEAN.   }   Aah!

MICK. How do you know all the old anti-British ones, Jean?

JEAN. Oh, I dunno, just pick 'em up. 'Ey – come on, don't try and get out of it.

LEN. Aye, come on, mate.

MICK. I'll give you an anti-British one.

JEAN. Yeah.

MICK. No offence . . ?

LEN. No, we can tek it, we can tek it. A good song's a good song, mate.

MICK (*sings*).

> 'Many years have rolled by
> Since the Irish Rebellion,
> When the guns of Britannia,
> They loudly did speak;
> When the bold I.R.A.
> Battled, shoulder to shoulder,
> And the blood from their bodies
> Flowed down Sackville Stree'.
>
> The forecourts of Dublin
> The English bombarded,
> Our spirit of freedom
> They tried hard to quell.

But amidst all the din
Came a voice, "No surrender!"
'Twas the voice of James Connolly,
The Irish rebel.

He went to his death
Like a true Son of Ireland,
The firing party
He bravely did face.
When the order rang out,
"Present Arms And Fire!",
James Connolly fell into
A ready-made grave.'

MICK *takes* DAWN's *hand.*

'God's curse on you, England,
You cruel-hearted monster,
Your deeds, they would shame
All the devils in Hell.
There are no flowers blooming,
But the shamrock is growing
On the grave of James Connolly,
The Irish rebel.'

And that's all you're gettin' off me.

LEN *claps.*

JEAN. Ooh, it was good, that, Mick.

LEN. Good song, mate, good song.

JEAN. Come on, you do one now, Dawn.

DAWN. Ooh, no!

LEN. Come on, Dawn.

MICK. No, come on.

DAWN. No.

LEN. Your turn now.

DAWN. I don't know no songs.

JEAN. 'Course you do.

DAWN (*suddenly, sings*). 'This is Number One,
    And the Party's just begun,

Roll me over,
Lay me down,
And do it again.'

ALL (*singing*). 'Roll me over
In the clover,
Roll me over,
Lay me down
And do it again!'

DAWN (*solo*). 'This is Number Two,
And the party's nearly through,
Roll me over,
Lay me down,
And do it again.'

ALL *sing chorus*.

DAWN (*solo*). 'This is Number Three,
And 'e's got me
On 'is knee –'

MICK *tickles* DAWN.

'Ey! (*Laughs*.)
'Roll me over,
Lay me down,
And do it again.'

ALL *sing chorus*.

DAWN (*solo*). 'This is Number Four
And 'e's got me
On the floor . . .'

MICK *picks* DAWN *up, and holds her down at floor level.*

'Ey! 'E's got me on the floor!
'Roll me over,
Lay me down,
And do it again.'

ALL *sing chorus*.

DAWN (*solo*). 'This is Number Five,
And 'e's mekkin'
A dirty dive . . .'

MICK *makes a dirty dive.*

'Roll me over,
Lay me down
And do it again.'

ALL *sing chorus.*

DAWN (*solo*). 'This is Number Six,
And 'e's got me in a fix,
Roll me over,
Lay me down – '

Blackout: total *darkness* . . .

MICK. } Oh.

LEN. } Ooh.

JEAN. } Blimey!

DAWN.   'Oo done that?

LEN. Oh, dear.

JEAN. It's the meter.

LEN. Oh.

DAWN. Oh, the meter's gone!

LEN. The meter's run out!

JEAN. I've got some 10p's 'ere somewhere.

LEN. Oh, dear.

MICK. Now's my chance to make my dirty dive.

DAWN *screams.*

LEN. Ey, oi!

DAWN. Sorry, Len.

LEN. Mind me.

DAWN. Did I land on ya?

LEN. No, it's alright, Dawn.

DAWN. I'm sorry.

LEN. No, you're alright.

JEAN. Blimey, I can't find 'em.

MICK. What is it you're looking for, Jean?

JEAN. I got some 10p's, I got me purse, 'ere somewhere.

MICK. Come 'ere, come 'ere, I have a handful of them here, look.

JEAN. I can't see your 'and.

LEN. It's alright, Jean, 'ere y'are, 'ere y'are, 'ang on.

LEN *strikes his lighter.*

JEAN. Oh, that's it; lovely. Thanks.

MICK. Got what you want?

JEAN *goes to the kitchen.*

JEAN. Yeah.

LEN. 'Ang on, Jean, I'll bring you a light.

The lighter goes out.

JEAN. I can't see a blind thing.

The darkness continues: MICK *assaults* DAWN. DAWN *screams. The lighter comes on again, by the meter.*

LEN. Can you see, Jean?

JEAN. Yeah, that's it.

DAWN. Stop it, Mick!

LEN. I'll put a couple more in, Jean, anyway.

JEAN. Well, that should be alright for a bit, Len.

LEN. No, we don't want it to 'appen again, do we?

JEAN. No.

DAWN. 'Ey, 'Ey, stop it . . . Jean, 'ere y'are, 'ave these.

JEAN. Len says 'e's putting some in.

DAWN. 'Be silly – 'ave them!

JEAN. Wait a minute, I'll 'ave a look, see if I've got any . . .

JEAN *looks in her purse.*

Look, I'll give you some 5p's for them, alright.

MICK. Put your money away, Jean, put your money away.

JEAN. Are you sure?

MICK. I am.

JEAN. Aye, alright. I'll put these on the telly. Thanks very much. You ain't robbing yourself, are you, Len?

The light comes on again.

LEN. No, no, Jean. I've just put a couple in. Keep us going for a while longer, anyway.

MICK. I dunno, I wasn't doing too bad in the dark, like.

DAWN. 'Ey – 'ey. Stop it! Dirty . . . I'm goin' on the toilet again.

JEAN. Alright.

DAWN (*going out*). Goes right through you, alco-hol.

JEAN. Once you start, you can't stop, can you?

LEN. You can't, can you?

    LEN *lights a cigarette.* MICK *takes a swig from* DAWN's *bottle of vodka.*

    Pause.

JEAN. I can't drink vodka.

MICK. No, 'tis horrible.

    Pause.

MICK. Not a bad old session, all the same.

LEN. No, no.

JEAN. Yeah. I like a singsong.

LEN. I do.

MICK. If you can't have a laugh and a drink on a Friday night, when can you?

JEAN. } Mmm.

LEN.   } Aye, that's right, mate.

MICK. A Saturday night!

    JEAN *laughs.*

LEN. Aye, Aye.

DAWN (*off*). Jean!

JEAN *gets up, and goes to the door.*

JEAN. What?

DAWN. Bring us some lavvy paper, will ya?

JEAN *finds a toilet roll in the kitchen.*

JEAN. Oh, cor blimey, it's run out again.

LEN. She get caught short?

JEAN (*going*). Yeah.

MICK. Having a quick Eartha Kitt.

Pause.

Very hard on the paper, our Dawn.

Pause.

LEN *laughs.*

Pause.

The following heard off, though hardly audible . . .

JEAN. Open the door.

DAWN. Oh, ta Jean.

JEAN. You can leave that in there.

DAWN. Ah, right, ta . . .

LEN *continues to laugh – he is considerably amused.*

MICK. Uh?

LEN (*still much amused*). Remember we used to say, 'Getting Up The Crack O' Dawn'?

MICK *is not amused.* LEN's *laughter dies away.*

MICK. Jesus Fuckin' Christ, man!

LEN. Oh, sorry, Mick.

Pause.

Sorry, mate.

MICK. Don't let her hear you saying that, she'd chew the fuckin' bollocks off you.

LEN. You're right, mate, aye.

JEAN *returns.*

MICK. Everything alright, Jean?

JEAN. Ooh, ah. Just stuck me 'ead outside the back door. Get a bit of fresh air. Think I feel worse now. 'T in' 'alf goin' cold out. (*She lights a cigarette.*) D'you know, I'm always putting toilet rolls in that toilet; I can't be bothered tekkin' one in wi' me, and bringing it back out again, I think that's a bit petty, don't you? So everybody just uses mine.

MICK. What are they like, the neighbours, alright?

JEAN. Yeah, well . . . well I never see 'em. 'Im next door 'e works at the Europa 'Otel, 'e's never in, 'im.

MICK. 'Tis just as well for him. He wouldn't have got much sleep with us tonight.

DAWN *returns, and sits on* MICK's *lap again.*

MICK. Alright, pet?

Pause.

DAWN. 'Ey, Mick, better watch the time, you know.

MICK. Eh, we're alright for a while yet. What did you say to Theresa?

DAWN. I told 'er we'd be late.

MICK. Ah, well, there y'are, you see, we're alright.

JEAN. Yeah, 't in' often you 'ave a night out, is it?

MICK. This is it, Jean.

DAWN. I feel sick, I do.

MICK. D' you wanna go out again?

DAWN. No. I'm pissed, you know.

DAWN *goes to the bed.*

MICK. We're all pissed.

DAWN. Gonna get me 'ead down, Jean.

MICK. Oh, no! Wait a minute, you. Jean, if she goes to sleep, you'll not get into bed tonight at all.

DAWN. No.

MICK. Hear when I'm talkin' to you – (*He gives her a light smack.*)

DAWN. You!

MICK. Don't go to sleep.

DAWN. I won't.

JEAN. Perhaps you ought to get a taxi.

MICK. Ah 'tis not worth it, Jean, all the distance.

JEAN. No.

MICK. Jes', I don't think you'd get one this time of the night, anyway.

DAWN. Oh, go on, gerra taxi.

MICK. I will in my bollocks. (*He gives her a prod.*)

DAWN. 'Ey, Mick.

MICK. You're walking home – don't go to sleep now, I'm in no condition to carry anyone.

Pause.

JEAN. What d'you think you'll be doing this weekend, Len?

LEN. I don't know – I thought I might go to the pictures. Daresay I'll 'ave a drink.

MICK. I suppose I'll have a couple of drinks meself this weekend.

Pause.

I'll be in my usual ole place, Len, tomorrow, if you feel like dropping in for a pint.

LEN. Oh right, right. Might see you there, then, Mick.

MICK. You know . . .

LEN. Aye.

Pause.

MICK. I haven't been to the pictures this year.

JEAN. No, nor me. D' you want a cup of coffee, Dawn?

MICK. You put your finger on it, there, Jean, now that's the very thing she needs.

DAWN. Eh?

JEAN. Cup of coffee.

DAWN. Ooh, ah.

JEAN. Yeah . . .

DAWN. I'll mek it, Jean.

> JEAN *holds out an empty cup to* DAWN.

JEAN. Alright then.

> *Pause. Then they all laugh.*

JEAN. Tell you what, when you've 'ad this coffee, you'll feel better then. You'll be able to start again, won't you?

DAWN. Yeah.

MICK. You will in my bollocks.

JEAN. 'Ey, there's plenty of stuff on 'ere, you know – just 'elp yourselves.

> JEAN *goes into the kitchen.*

LEN. Oh, aye.

MICK. I have an old jar sitting there somewhere, Len.

LEN. Oh, aye . . .

MICK. Would you ever throw it over to me, like?

LEN. 'Ere y'are, mate.

MICK. Thanks very much.

LEN. There's some in there.

> *Pause.*

DAWN. What 'appened to you, Len?

LEN. Eh?

DAWN. Eh? What 'appened to you?

LEN. What d'you mean, like?

DAWN. When you went away, never come back?

MICK. Ar, for Jes' sake.

LEN. Oh, oh.

DAWN. Why d'you disappear that Christmas? We didn't know where you was. Did we upset ya? Did we? Eh? Was yer upset?

MICK. Ar, go to sleep will you?

LEN. Ar, no, no . . . what it was, I went up 'ome that Christmas, and there was a job going, so I took it – You've got to go where the jobs are, 'aven't you?

MICK. You got to go where the work is, Len.

LEN. Aye.

MICK. He was probably a bit homesick and all – you were a bit homesick, Len?

LEN. Agh, long time ago, mate: can't remember.

MICK. I know what it's like. I'd work at home if I could, but there's nothing there – I'd be sitting on my arse all day.

DAWN. Country boys, ent ya?

MICK. Country boys at heart.

LEN. Aye; aye.

DAWN. You two.

JEAN. I couldn't live in the country, me.

MICK. 'T's not everyone's cup o' tea, Jean. There's fuck all in it. I couldn't get out of it quick enough.

JEAN. Be too quiet for me.

LEN. No – best place.

JEAN. Yeah, you like it, don't you Len?

LEN. I do, I do.

DAWN. We missed you, though, Len. Didn't we, Mick? Jean?

MICK. He doesn't need me to tell him that.

DAWN. Jean: didn't we miss 'im?

JEAN. Ooh, ah, yeah, listen, d'you think you ought to 'ave this coffee black?

MICK. Aw, black is right.

DAWN. No. No, Jean.

JEAN. Are you sure?

DAWN. Ooh ah.

JEAN. Alright, then, I got a drop of milk.

DAWN. Spot of milk, Jean.

LEN. Are you working tomorrow, then, Jean?

JEAN. Oh yeah, Len, I work every Sat'day now.

LEN. 'Ope you 'aven't got an early start?

JEAN. Well, I've got to be up at seven, 'cos me shift's eight till four, see?

MICK. Aw, Jes' Christ, that's early enough for you.

LEN. It is, it is.

JEAN. Oh, it's alright, I don't mind, I can do it dead easy, 'cos I don't need a lot of sleep, see?

LEN. 'Ow d'you find working there again, then, Jean, after all this time?

JEAN. Well, it ain't the same, Len. 'Cos, you know, it's gone self-service up there now.

LEN. Aye.

JEAN. And you know, they give us these instructions, we're not allowed to touch the pumps.

LEN. Mm.

JEAN. I mean, it's ludicrous, really, when you consider the number of garages I've worked in. Still, never mind – it's 'andy to run to work if ever I 'ave to.

LEN. Aye.

JEAN. I'll just come by 'ere.

LEN. Sorry, Jean – 'ere you go.

JEAN (*handing* DAWN *a coffee*): 'Ere y'are. T's 'ot.

MICK. There ye are, Missus.

DAWN. Ooh, ah. Lovely.

JEAN. D'you wanna sit there a bit, Len?

LEN. No, no, I'm alright there, Jean, don't worry about me.

JEAN. No, I wish you would, really, 'cos I'm gettin' a bit 'ot by that.

LEN. Are you sure?

JEAN. Yeah.

LEN. Right-o, say the word if you want to come back, like.

JEAN (*getting out a cigarette*). No, you're alright. Oh, you've got one on?

LEN. Aye. Thank you.

JEAN *takes off her cardigan.*

JEAN. Ooh, ah, I used to love it on them pumps, you know. Specially in the summer. We used to get the chairs out on the forecourt, do a bit of sunbathing.

LEN. Ah.

JEAN. I loved it. I used to be black, I 'ad.

LEN. Ha.

JEAN. We used to go out and get a cuppa tea, or a paper, and bring it back with yer, if you're a bit slack, like, you know.

LEN. Aye.

JEAN. Or sometimes we'd go out, we'd get 'alf a melon, bottle of beer, anything . . .

LEN. Ah.

JEAN. But of course it's a different job altogether now. I'm just stuck there be'ind the till, see? 'Cos I liked it when you could get out a bit, and you could 'ave a chat to people while you're filling them up with petrol.

LEN. Uh?

JEAN. But now, they just come in, they give me the money, I give 'em the change, and that's it.

LEN. Ar.

JEAN. And you know, when they modernised this, up 'ere, they twisted it all round, y'know – the pumps are on the side now.

LEN. 'Course they are, that's right.

JEAN. Yeah, whereas they were on the front before. So I've got me back to the 'Igh Road, I just stare at a bloody brick wall all day. Still, ne' mind – pays the rent, dunnit?

Short pause.

LEN. Is it that same couple running it, then?

JEAN. What couple?

LEN. That couple as ran it when you used to work there.

JEAN. There was only the Manager, Sid.

LEN. Aye. An' 'is wife.

JEAN. 'Is wife d'ain't work there.

LEN. Din't she?

JEAN. No. There was only me, Sid and Dolly.

LEN. Dolly, Dolly.

JEAN. Dolly weren't 'is wife.

LEN. Wa'n't she?

JEAN. No. You're getting confused 'cos Dolly was at Sid's Leaving Party that we went to, d'you remember?

LEN. Oh aye.

JEAN. Yeah.

LEN. Wa'n't she 'is wife?

JEAN. No.

LEN. Oh.

Pause.

'Oo's running it now, then?

DAWN (*half asleep*). Pakis, Len. Pakis running it.

LEN. Are they?

DAWN. Yeah.

JEAN. Yeah.

LEN. Treat you alright, do they?

JEAN. Yeah, why?

LEN. Lucky.

JEAN. Am I?

DAWN. Don't trust 'em, I don't.

LEN. Gettin' in everywhere now, aren't they? They want to go back where they came from.

JEAN. We'd all be in a sorry state then, wouldn't we? The 'ospitals 'd shut down, the buses'd come off –

LEN. Solve the unemployment problem, wouldn't it?

JEAN. Ah, but they do a lot of jobs that white people wouldn't touch.

MICK. Ah, now you've put your finger on it, Jean: that's right enough.

LEN. I s'pose there's something in that, aye.

DAWN. Bleedin' bus condustress yesterday, Jean's big, black piece 'er was; 'ad the babby wi'me, push-chair, bags; I said to 'er, "Scuse me, will yer ding the bell for me please, because I wanna geroff at Willesden Lane.' Did 'er fuck ding the bell, Jean. Nearly ended up in bleedin' Cricklewood, I did. Give 'er a mouthful. Told 'er where to geroff. Jungle.

JEAN. It in't 'cos 'er's black; I mean, I know a lot of white bus condustresses'd do that to you.

DAWN. No . . . they'm lazy buggers, they am.

MICK. Ah, no. Fair do's, now. I've worked with them, on the sites – like yourself, Len. Some of them are very hard workers. Big fuckin' bastards, an' all.

LEN. Oh, the West Indians are alright.

MICK. Ah, yeah – 'tis the fucking Scotchies I can't stick.

JEAN. Oh, well, we're all the same underneath, in't we?

LEN. Ar, but the thing about the Pakis is, they don't try to change their ways – they don't try to fit in.

JEAN. Would you try an' fit in with them, if you went over there?

LEN. Aye.

JEAN. Would ya?

LEN. Aye.

JEAN. You'd eat all the same food, curries an' all that, you'd live in the same conditions?

LEN. No.

JEAN. Oh, you're saying you wouldn't fit in?

LEN. I wouldn't live like them.

JEAN. But you expect them to live like you when they come over 'ere?

LEN. Aye – that's different, int it?

JEAN. Oh, is it? What's different about it?

LEN. Well, 'oo'd want to live the way they live?

JEAN. D'you know 'ow they live?

LEN. Aye.

JEAN. Ow?

LEN. Well . . .

JEAN. Eh?

LEN. Well . . . you know . . .

JEAN. Yeah, I know – I just wondered if you knew.

Long pause.

MICK. I had a curry the other night. I don't know how they take it. Went right through me. I could've shat through the eye of a needle.

Pause.

Funny the way you never see a Pak in a pub, like.

JEAN. Well, that's 'cos some of them are Moslems, see, an' er, it's against their religion to drink.

MICK. Oh, I get it.

JEAN (*gets out cigarettes*): One o'these, Dawn? Oh, look at 'er – 'er's gone, in 'er?

DAWN *is asleep.*

MICK. She's away with the band.

JEAN. Len?

LEN. Can you spare it?

JEAN. Yeah.

LEN. Oh. Don't mind if I do, Jean, thank you.

> *He lights* JEAN's *cigarette.*

> 'Ere y'are.

> *Pause.*

JEAN. 'Ave you been anywhere nice, Len, in the car, since you've been down 'ere?

LEN. Oh, no.

MICK. D'you know what, Jean?

JEAN. Mm?

MICK. This man has offered to take the kiddies for a run in the jamjar.

JEAN. Oh, ah, they'll love that, Len.

MICK. They'll love that.

LEN. Take 'em off your 'ands, like.

MICK. You've the heart of a lion, boy. They're a terrible handful.

JEAN. Where you going to tek 'em, Len?

LEN. Oh, thought I might go to the zoo, like.

JEAN. Oh, ah, they'll love that, won't they, going to the zoo?

MICK. They'll love that.

JEAN. Not so long back, you know, I took 'em to a funfair. 'Course, they wanted to go on everything, so I 'ad to go on everything with 'em – I was terrified, me.

MICK. They're a terrible shower of gangsters. They hunt in packs.

> MICK *goes out.*

> *Pause.* DAWN *is still asleep.*

JEAN. Ooh, ah, they'll love that, Len, going out in the car.

Pause.

LEN. Well – better start thinking about going.

JEAN. What sort of car you got?

LEN. Cortina.

JEAN. Oh, ah, they're nice, en' they?

LEN. Aye, it's a bit old, this'n, it's still a runner, like.

Pause.

JEAN. Good job you ain't driving tonight.

LEN. Aye, huh.

Pause.

JEAN. Well, you'll 'ave to come down the garage, get some petrol off me.

LEN. Aye, I will, huh.

Pause.

JEAN. 'Er's going to 'ave an 'ead on 'er tomorrow, en 'er?

LEN *laughs.*

JEAN. D'you wan' a cup o' coffee, Len?

LEN. No. No, I'll be off in a minute, Jean.

JEAN. You can stop if you want.

Very long pause.

MICK *returns, whistling quietly to himself. He tests a couple of cans, then goes over to* DAWN, *and smacks her bottom.*

DAWN. Ow. Don't.

MICK. Come on, Missus, time to go time.

DAWN. Silly.

DAWN *goes back to sleep.*

MICK *returns to examine the beer cans at the table.*

MICK. There's a drop left in here, Len: d'you want some?

LEN. Oh, aye, finish it off, like.

MICK. What about you, Jean?

JEAN. No, I'm alright.

MICK. Are you sure?

JEAN. Mm.

MICK. Oh, Jes', you look a bit tired, girl. I'll tell you what, I'll get this woman shifted, and then you can have a lie down to yourself.

(MICK *touches* DAWN*'s stockinged foot. She jumps, and bangs her head on the headboard*).

DAWN. Ooh, blimey, Mick!

MICK. What's wrong with you?

DAWN. Made me bump my bleedin' 'ead, you did.

MICK. Egh, you're alright!

DAWN. Ooh.

MICK. Come on!

DAWN. 'Ey!

MICK. Come on, it's time to get up.

DAWN. Don't be rough with me!

MICK. Well, we have to go, like.

DAWN. I know – I'm ready, en' I?

MICK. Alright, then.

DAWN. Silly. (*She lies down again.*)

MICK. Two minutes. I'll give you two minutes. (MICK *returns to the table, and the drinks.*) Are you walking up the road, Len?

Pause.

Uh?

DAWN *gets up.*

DAWN. I'm tired.

MICK. Are you sick?

DAWN. No. (*She goes out, to the loo.*)

MICK. Yeah – well, don't be all night.

Pause. LEN *and* JEAN *say nothing and do nothing.* MICK *faces the drinks, and sings the following in a relaxed, intermittent kind of way, and drinks a bit.*

MICK (*sings*). 'Hairy eggs and bacon,
    Hairy eggs and ham!
    Hairy eggs and bacon,
    Hairy eggs and ham!
    Hairy eggs and bacon,
    Hairy eggs and ham!
    Hairy eggs and bacon,
    Hairy eggs and ham!'

    DAWN *comes back.*

DAWN. Come on Mick, chop-chop.

MICK. I'll just knock this back.

DAWN. 'Er'll be wondering where we am, Theresa. Eh? Ooh, blimey, Jean, you'll 'ave us 'ere all bleedin' night at this rate. Where's my shoes? Ooh ah, I've gorrem: no – there they am. (*She puts on her shoes.*)

MICK. Uh, we did a bit of damage here tonight.

LEN. Aye.

DAWN. I want no rows with Theresa, Mick.

MICK. Ach.

DAWN. Funny bugger, 'er, you know. Couldn't be doin' with it, I couldn't. (*Quietly, to* JEAN.) Alright, am yer, Jean?

JEAN. Yeah, yeah.

DAWN. Alright am yer, Len?

LEN. Aye.

DAWN. Yeah – lovely to see ya.

LEN. Aye – nice to see you, Dawn.

MICK. Now here, Missus, don't be making yourself comfortable.

DAWN. 'Course I ain't.

MICK. Ar, you're not putting on make-up this time of night?

DAWN. Got to walk up the 'Igh Road, en I?

MICK. Who the fuck'll be looking at you?

DAWN. Heh, you don't know, do you? Only a bit o' lippy, any road.

MICK. You're all lip. Jean.

JEAN. Mm?

MICK. Very nice.

JEAN. Yeah.

MICK. Thanks very much. Grand old session.

JEAN. Yeah.

MICK. Ha? Bit of an old singsong.

JEAN. Yeah.

MICK. Aw, lovely.

JEAN. Yeah.

MICK *rubs the back of* JEAN's *head.*

MICK. We won't let it be so long again.

JEAN. No.

DAWN. Come round next week, Jean.

JEAN. Yeah, I will.

DAWN. Lovely night, Jean.

JEAN. Yeah.

DAWN. Lovely. Enjoyed yourself?

JEAN. Yeah, I 'ave.

DAWN. 'Course you 'ave. Want to get out more often, you do, Jean, you know – you do – 't en't good, stoppin' in, ooh no. Enjoyed myself, any road. Lovely! Enjoyed myself! Know where we live, Len!

———————————————

(The following dialogue runs simultaneously with the preceding passage, and begins after: 'Yeah, I will.')

MICK. Len: put it there, baby. No fuckin' problems.

LEN. No.

MICK. Okay?

LEN. Right-o, mate.

MICK. I'll be at my usual old station tomorrow.

LEN. Right-o.

MICK. If you feel like dropping in for a pint.

LEN. Right.

MICK. If I don't see you tomorrow, I'll see you through the week.

LEN. Okay, mate, right. Right.

DAWN (concluding). Know where we live, Len!

LEN. Aye.

MICK. Thanks for the ole soup, Jean.

JEAN. Yeah.

DAWN. Don't forget to come round, Jean.

JEAN. Yeah, I will next week.

DAWN. Babbies am askin' for you, you know.

MICK. Oh, Dawn –

DAWN. Eh?

MICK. D'you remember the old Baby Bellings?

DAWN. Ooh, blimey. Don't.

MICK. We had one of them in Messina.

DAWN. We did.

MICK. D'you remember that Christmas?

DAWN. Ooh, ah! Twenty-nine pound turkey 'e brought 'ome, Len, six pound 'o sausages.

MICK. You see, the way it was, Len, I got caught up in the pub on Christmas Eve, and by the time I got to the butcher, the only thing he had left was about the size of a pig. Lord Jesus, you could've stuffed the turkey with the Baby Belling.

DAWN. I nearly killed 'im, I did, Len. You 'ad to break in upstairs.

MICK. We did an' all; I put my shoulder to the door of the flat upstairs; the fellow was away for Christmas, like, you know.

DAWN. You remember that, Jean, you was there, I was out 'ere with Tracy.

JEAN. Yeah.

MICK. She was there. 'Twas a very nice bird, anyway.

DAWN. Lovely bird.

MICK. Come on, Missus.

DAWN. Ooh – we'm goin'.

MICK. Time to go – you got to carry me home now!

DAWN. Ooh ah!

MICK. See that, Len? I get carried home.

LEN. Oh, aye. Aye.

MICK. Jean: very nice. Thanks very much. No fuckin' problems.

LEN. Tara then. Tara Dawn.

DAWN. See you. See you, Jean.

JEAN. Tara.

MICK. I'll see you, Len.

LEN. Tara mate, all the best like.

MICK. Ooh, for Jesus' sake.

DAWN. Ooh, blimey, Mick – I can't carry you.

MICK. Aw, go on – ah?

DAWN. Do me flippin' back in, you.

MICK. Oh Jesus Christ. Jes', tis dark.

DAWN. Ooh blimey! Ah.

MICK. Put that light on there, will you?

DAWN. Aye. 'Ey, don't forget to open this door quiet, now.

MICK. Okay.

DAWN. Shut it quiet 'cos you'll wake the 'ouse up.

MICK. Alright, no fuckin' problems. Jes', 'tis fuckin' chilly.

DAWN Ooh ah.

MICK. Come here.

DAWN. Yeah.

> MICK *and* DAWN *have faded away down the street.*
>
> *Silence: a long pause. Then . . .*

LEN. Surprised to see you again.

JEAN. Yeah. Surprise to you, an' all.

> LEN *laughs.*
>
> *Pause.*

LEN. They don't change, them two, do they?

JEAN. No – no, they don't.

> *Pause.*

LEN (*belches*). Oh – I beg your pardon, Jean.

JEAN (*gets out cigarettes*). One of these, Len?

LEN. Oh, I don't mind if I do, Jean, thank you. 'Ere y'are.

> LEN *lights* JEAN's *cigarette.*
>
> *Pause.*

LEN (*getting up*). Look, Jean, I think I ought to go really – y'know . . .

JEAN. Oh no, you don't 'ave to.

LEN. No, you've got to get up early in the morning.

JEAN. Oh well, that don't matter.

> *Pause.*

LEN. You don't want me to stay.

JEAN. Yes, yes I do. I mean, 'ave another drink if you want.

LEN. No, I've got, I've got some 'ere.

JEAN. Well, 'ave a top-up then, or summat.

LEN. No, I've 'ad enough to drink.

JEAN. Yeah, well . . . praps we all 'ave, eh?

LEN. Aye.

Pause.

LEN. She's a character, is Dawn, isn't she?

JEAN. Yeah. Yeah, 'er is. 'S been a good friend to me, 'er 'as.

LEN. Aye.

> JEAN *starts to cry, quietly, and with her head down.*

What's up?

> LEN *gets up, and puts his cup down.*

Eh?

> *He puts his arm round* JEAN, *and takes it away almost immediately.*

What's the matter?

JEAN. Just pleased to see you, that's all.

LEN Oh! (*Laughing.*) Eh?

> *He hugs her.*

Ah! Eh? That's better. Nothing to cry about.

> *He stands up.* JEAN *starts to cry again at the same time.* LEN *bends down again to put his arm round her, gets a bit stuck, and stands up. He puts out his cigarette, and he takes her cigarette, and puts that out. Then he crouches down, and hugs* JEAN.

LEN. We've all 'ad a lot to drink tonight, that's all.

JEAN (*crying*). But I drink all the time.

> JEAN *cries throughout the following, never raising her head from her lap. And somewhere during this speech,* LEN *starts to cry, too.*

I just sit 'ere. I didn't enjoy meself tonight. Didn't want to talk about anything, just got upset. There was . . . there was a bloke 'ere earlier . . . an' em . . . Dawn was 'ere, an', uh . . . 'is wife came, an' that's 'ow the bed broke . . . I don't even like 'im. I don't tell 'er anything.

> *Pause.*

I 'ate living 'ere. She thinks I don't go out with anybody. An' I do. Well, I never like 'em. They don't like me, they just like 'itting me.

Pause.

I've been pregnant.

Pause.

I've always 'ad to get rid of 'em on me own.

Pause.

When she was 'avin' 'ers, I was 'aving mine. I lie to 'er all the time. I just want to die.

LEN *is still crying, and hugging* JEAN. *He stands up suddenly.*

LEN. Me leg's gone to sleep.

JEAN. I'm 'ot.

LEN. Shall I put the fire off?

JEAN. No.

LEN. D'you want a cup of coffee?

JEAN. No. Just didn't think.

LEN. Eh?

JEAN. I was big-'eaded.

LEN. What about?

JEAN. I was always 'orrible to you.

JEAN *moves to the bed, and lies on it, continuing to keep her face away from* LEN.

LEN. Eh?

JEAN. You were nice to me and, em . . . I just wanted to 'ave a good time . . . stupid.

Pause.

LEN *crouches down by her, and hugs her for a few moments. Then he separates.*

LEN. You ought to go to bed.

JEAN. No point in going to bed now. I'll just sleep 'ere.

LEN. D'you want me to go?

Pause.

JEAN. 'Don't mind.

LEN. I'll stay if you want.

Pause.

You go to bed – I'll sleep in the chair.

JEAN. You'll 'ave to 'ave a blanket.

LEN. I'll be alright.

JEAN. It goes cold in the night.

LEN. I'll be alright.

Pause.

I've got me coat. Come on.

JEAN *sits up.*

JEAN. In' it a mess in 'ere?

LEN. Aye. (*He puts his coat on the armchair, and takes off his jacket.*) I'll just go to the toilet.

JEAN. Will you put the big light off? Just there.

LEN. Oh, aye.

LEN *goes out.* JEAN *throws a cushion and the counterpane from her bed onto the armchair. Then she undresses.* LEN *returns at a moment when she happens to be naked from the waist upward. Neither of them are at all bothered by this: each takes the other's presence in these circumstances for granted.* LEN *picks up the counterpane.*

LEN. Will it be alright if I 'ave this?

JEAN. Yeah. Yeah.

LEN *takes off his shoes.* JEAN *gets into bed.* LEN *prepares the armchair.*

JEAN. You can leave that fire on, 'cos it'll go off when the meter runs out.

LEN. Shall I put that light out?

JEAN. Yeah.

LEN *goes towards the bedside lamp. He sits on* JEAN's *bed.*

Pause.

LEN. You alright?

JEAN. Yeah.

LEN. Good night.

He kisses her, gently and briefly. Then he puts out the light, and finds his way back to the chair, lit by the electric fire. He settles in the chair, gathering the counterpane and coat round him.

Long pause.

Slow fade to blackout.

The End

Songs

DANNY BOY

I KNEW A FARMER

I knew a far-mer, and I knew 'im well. I knew 'is daugh-ter and 'er name was Nell. She was so pret-ty and on-ly six-teen, And I showed 'er the works of my thresh-ing mach-ine.

CHORUS

I 'ad 'er, I 'ad 'er, I 'ad 'er, I 'ay. I 'ad 'er, I 'ad 'er, I showed 'er the way. They were the best days of my life, I would say, And I spent them a-lead-ing young mai-dens a-stray.

IT'S THE SAME THE WHOLE WORLD OVER

WHEN I WAS YOUNG, I USED TO BE

MANY YEARS HAVE ROLLED BY SINCE THE IRISH REBELLION

ROLL ME OVER

HAIRY EGGS AND BACON

Hair-y eggs and bac-on, Hair-y eggs and ham!
Hair-y eggs and bac-on, Hair-y eggs and ham!
Hair-y eggs and bac-on, Hair-y eggs and ham!
Hair-y eggs and bac-on, Hair-y eggs and ham!